The Historical NEVADA MAGAZINE

Outstanding Historical Features
From the Pages of *Nevada Magazine*

Published by

NEVADA
M A G A Z I N E

A Division of the Nevada Commission on Tourism
Carson City and Las Vegas, Nevada

Cover and book design by Denise Barr

Copyright 1998 by
Nevada Magazine
401 N. Carson St., Suite 100
Carson City, Nevada 89701-4291.

First Printing, 1998.

All Rights Reserved.

Printed in the U.S.A.

ISBN 1-890136-06-9

Cover Photograph

This photograph of the Wild Bunch is part of the myth and mystery surrounding the robbery of the First National Bank of Winnemucca in September 1900. According to the legend, which has been discredited, following the robbery the photo was sent to the bank's owner with a thank-you note. Outlaws in the photo are, from left, Harry Longabaugh (a.k.a. the Sundance Kid), Bill Carver, Ben Kilpatrick (the Tall Texan), Harvey Logan (Kid Curry), and Robert LeRoy Parker (Butch Cassidy). Photo courtesy of the Western History Collection, Denver Public Library.

Dedicated to
Fred Greulich, Don Bowers, and C.J. Hadley

TABLE OF CONTENTS

INTRODUCTION

How do you decide what to include in a book compiling outstanding historical stories that have appeared in *Nevada Magazine* during the past six decades? The task wasn't easy because there have been so many articles devoted to Nevada's rich and colorful past. The stories featured here represent the kind of colorful features that have appeared in *Nevada Magazine.* They include works by many of the state's most talented historians and writers. In a few cases, the articles broke new ground by revealing previously unknown facts about an intriguing historical person or event.

Among the features included in this volume are:

"Mornin' on the Desert" is a poem that was found on the door of a cabin in Southern Nevada. This bit of verse appeared in *Nevada Highways and Parks,* which was *Nevada Magazine's* original name, in 1936.

"Princes of the Fourth Estate" by frequent *Nevada Magazine* contributor David W. Toll, whose first story for *Nevada Magazine* appeared in 1966, is an engaging look at Mark Twain, Dan De Quille, and the glory days of Comstock journalism. The story appeared in the Winter 1979 issue.

"Nevada's First Woman Sheriff" by Craig MacDonald is a revealing look at the life of Clara Dunham Crowell, who in 1919 was appointed sheriff of Lander County. The article appeared in January/February 1981.

"Butch Cassidy and the Great Winnemucca Bank Robbery" by David W. Toll, first published in May/June 1983, debunks the popular myth that Butch Cassidy and the Sundance Kid robbed the First National Bank of Winnemucca in 1900.

"Petticoat Prospectors" by Terri Sprenger-Farley, who has written several historical novels about Nevada, is a fascinating look at a frequently overlooked class of Nevada miners—women. The article, which appeared in November/December 1983, describes a handful of women prospectors who ignored the hardships and made their mark on the state.

~

"Queen of Tarts" by Susan James is a study of the life and death of Julia Bulette, a Virginia City prostitute who was brutally murdered in 1867. Although some 20th-century writers recrafted Bulette's story, elevating her to the status of folk heroine and portraying her as a wealthy courtesan with a heart of gold, James shows that she was neither wealthy nor particularly charitable. The story appeared in September/October 1984.

~

"The Great Train Robbery" by Terri Sprenger-Farley tells the story of the first train robbery committed in the West, which took place between Reno and Verdi in 1870. The article was published in May/June 1986.

~

"Gunfighters of Pioche" by A.D. Hopkins, a veteran Las Vegas journalist, describes some of the gunmen, thugs, and thieves who helped the mining camp of Pioche earn its reputation as the most violent town in the West in the 1870s. The story appeared in September/October 1986.

~

"Ghost Town Rambler" by Richard Moreno offers an overview of many of Nevada's most picturesque and historic ghost towns including Goldfield, Gold Point, Unionville, and Belmont. The article appeared in the May/June 1988 issue.

~

"The First Black Rancher" by Ed Johnson and Elmer R. Rusco reveals the important role that African-American ranchers, such as Ben Palmer, played in the settling of the

Carson Valley. Johnson is author of *Walker River Paiutes: A Tribal History,* and Rusco is author of *Good Times Coming? Black Nevadans in the 19th Century.* The article was published in January/February 1989.

~*~

"Dat So La Lee and the Myth Weavers" by Reno writer Christopher Ross describes the unique relationship between legendary Washoe basketmaker Dat So La Lee and Carson City businessman Abe Cohn and his wife, Amy. The story appeared in September/October 1989.

~*~

"Gass' Station" by Ralph J. Roske and Michael S. Green explores the life of Octavius Decatur Gass, who started a ranch in the Las Vegas Valley in 1864, making him the first permanent settler in the area. The late Ralph Roske was professor emeritus of history of the University of Nevada, Las Vegas. Green is a history instructor at the Community College of Southern Nevada. The article appeared in September/October 1989.

~*~

"Rail Daze" by Phillip I. Earl offers a brief overview of the Carson & Colorado Railroad, which was located in such a remote region of Nevada and California that it was said to be either 300 miles too long or 300 years too early. Earl is curator of history at the Nevada Historical Society and a frequent *Nevada Magazine* contributor. The story appeared in the Nevada 125th Anniversary Issue in October 1989.

~*~

"Where's the Beef?" by Howard Hickson, the former director of Elko's Northeastern Nevada Museum, recalls a creative cattle rustler who, in the 1920s, perplexed authorities trying to follow his tracks by wearing shoes that had cattle-hoof soles. The article appeared in January/February 1990.

~*~

"Nevada's Historic Architect" by Ronald M. James, Nevada's

state historic preservation officer, presents a profile of Frederic J. DeLongchamps, the Reno architect who designed seven Nevada courthouses as well as numerous homes, schools, and public buildings. The story appeared in July/August 1994.

~

"Ten Historic Performances" by Richard Moreno lists history-making performances that occurred in Nevada. The events include the first meeting of the Rat Pack at the Sands Hotel in Las Vegas in January 1960 and the night bandleader Ted Lewis performed at Elko's Commercial Hotel in 1941, which was the first time a casino offered big-name entertainment. The article appeared in January/February 1995.

~

"Leading Ladies" by Dana R. Bennett recalls Nevada's first women legislators, Sadie Hurst of Reno and Frances Friedhoff of Yerington. Bennett, a former research analyst with the Nevada State Legislature, tells how Hurst became the state's first female member of the Assembly in 1919 and how Friedhoff was appointed the first woman member of the State Senate in 1935. The story appeared in March/April 1995.

~

"How Nevada Became 'Nevada'" by Guy Louis Rocha describes the evolution of the state's name in the 1850s and 1860s. Rocha, who is Nevada's state archivist, uncovers the reason Nevada (Spanish for "snow-covered") was selected over other choices such as Esmeralda, Oro Plata, and Washoe. The essay appeared in March/April 1996.—*Richard Moreno*

NEVADA MAGAZINE: THE EARLY YEARS

How two Nevada highway men sent the magazine on a 60-year joyride.

When the first issue of *Nevada Magazine* appeared in January 1936, Hoover Dam was less than a year old, Franklin Delano Roosevelt was president, and the state's population had just passed 100,000. Nevada had 2,100 miles of surfaced roads—and couldn't wait to tell the world.

The magazine was originally called *Nevada Highways and Parks*. It was published by the Nevada Department of Highways, and one of its primary jobs was to tell people that the state had good roads.

The publication contained no advertising and was free to tourists. Produced on a shoestring, it was edited by Fred Greulich, who doubled as the highway department publicist, and printed in black and white by the State Printing Office in Carson City.

Exactly how the magazine came about isn't clear, but old-timers recall that Greulich either suggested creating the magazine or was given the job by former State Highway Engineer Robert A. Allen.

Greulich worked in a cramped office in the Heroes Memorial Building near the State Capital. During his 20 years on the job, he wrote virtually every article that appeared in *Nevada Highways and Parks*. He cajoled highway department photographers, who were more accustomed to snapping pictures of new bridges and roads, to shoot landscapes, parks, ghost towns, and dams.

The timing of the magazine's appearance was fortuitous. The 1930s was a dynamic decade in Nevada. Americans had discovered the automobile and the thrill of driving open roads—of which Nevada has always had plenty—and the federal government was trying to help America recover from the Great Depression. Projects included the construction of Hoover Dam, creation of jobs by the Works Progress Administration, and New Deal road-building programs.

Nevada lawmakers did their part to stimulate the state's development. In the '30s, divorce laws were loosened, gambling was made legal, better roads were built, and the legislature created both the Nevada State Park System and the Nevada State Museum—actions aimed at attracting more visitors to the state.

Meanwhile, other Western states saw the importance of tourism. Numerous state publications appeared in the 1920s and '30s, including *New Mexico* (1923), *Arizona Highways* (1925), *Colorado Outdoors* (1938), and *Texas Parks and Wildlife* (1938).

Producing the bimonthly (later quarterly) magazine was an ideal assignment for Greulich, a former telegrapher who enjoyed exploring the state's back roads and mines.

Greulich shared his vision of Nevada in the first issue when he wrote that he hoped the magazine "will serve a useful purpose in disseminating facts and news about Nevada's highways and parks, its abundant natural scenic places, and perhaps promote a wider knowledge of its mountains, deserts, and the real western, friendly spirit of its people."

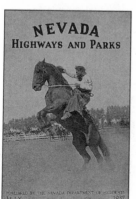

Some subjects, though, were off-limits. For the magazine's first 17 years, gambling and divorce weren't mentioned at all. Adrian Atwater, who in the early 1950s became the first highway department photographer assigned to the magazine, recalled that those two subjects were "discouraged" because officials felt they did not present a positive image for the state. Road construction and mining, however, were welcome topics.

"Fred loved mining. There was never a trip that he didn't bring back a bag of ore samples," Atwater said.

"In those days, Fred and I were a two-man team. He did all the writing, and I did all the photography. One week each month we'd travel the state together to do stories."

Atwater describes Greulich as "a fine old gentleman, well groomed, well spoken, with a good sense of humor. I never heard him swear." He says Greulich, a quiet, formal man, always wore a coat and tie, even when traveling in remote parts of the state.

World War II temporarily shut down the magazine. Paper shortages during the war years meant that promotional publications like *Nevada Highways and Parks* couldn't be published. But the magazine returned in January 1946 with a Greulich-written lead feature proclaiming, "Nevada Tourist Roads Are Calling You."

America was ready for change in the postwar years, and *Nevada Highways and Parks* changed along with it. The magazine began using color photography as well as more, and larger, pages. Stories highlighted the state's growing cities, towns, and industries. The magazine was published irregularly. At least two issues appeared per year, and in some years as many as four were printed. The magazine was mailed free to tourists asking for information about the state.

Two issues in 1953 were noteworthy. In January, Greulich finally acknowledged the phenomenal growth of Las Vegas and put a daytime photo of Fremont Street on the cover—the first time readers were allowed to glimpse casinos. Inside, the magazine featured night shots of Las Vegas and Reno.

The December 1953 issue was the most unusual in the magazine's history. The cover showed a mushroom cloud rising above the Southern Nevada desert, and atomic testing was the subject of the lead story, "Operation Doom Town."

Reflecting attitudes of the times, stories focused on how atomic testing in Nevada helped to keep America strong and safe.

In the January 1956 issue readers finally saw the man who had been responsible for the magazine for two decades. On the inside cover was a tiny photo of a smiling, bespectacled man at a typewriter. An editor's note explained that Fred Greulich was retiring after having produced 52 issues.

Replacing Greulich was Donald L. Bowers, former chief of the *Fallon Eagle.* Bowers, a native of Fallon, had served in the Navy during World War II and following the war edited an English-language magazine in Russia. While maintaining much of the look established by Greulich, Bowers made subtle changes. He introduced shorter articles, modern page designs, a new masthead, and features about events and historical Nevada characters like Mark Twain and Hank Monk.

"Don knew a lot about magazines," recalled veteran Nevada journalist Guy Shipler, who contributed to the magazine during Bower's tenure. "My recollection is that he was a good editor.

"I think he was more responsible than anyone else for turning the magazine from a highway brochure to an honest-to-god magazine."

Shipler and others describe Bowers as a free-thinking intellectual who was well read, well traveled, and well connected.

"He seemed to know everyone in the state," recalled David Moore, *Nevada Magazine's* current editor, who was hired by Bowers in the early 1970s as a circulation gofer. "He really liked traveling around the state, particularly to places like Austin and Eureka."

In 1964, Bowers introduced his most sweeping changes. He persuaded the legislature to allow him to convert the free publication into one with a paid circulation, advertising, and national distribution. The first issue of the new *Nevada Magazine,* as most people called it, was a special commemorative Centennial edition. The 68-page magazine—the largest issue produced to that time—carried a 50-cent price tag and a message from Bowers: "This special issue of *Nevada Highways & Parks* marks our Centennial . . . and also another transition . . . A new, bigger *Nevada Magazine*. Costs you a little but brings you much more." The subscription price was $2 for four issues.

In 1975, after 20 years as editor, Bowers retired. His successor was Judy Casey, who had served as managing editor for five years. A few issues later, Casey became a highway department publicist and was followed by Caroline J. Hadley, a former managing editor of *Car and Driver*. Coinciding with Hadley's arrival were other changes. The magazine moved from the Department of Highways to the Department of Economic Development and later the Nevada Commission on Tourism. The name was officially shortened to *Nevada Magazine*, and, in 1979, frequency was increased to six times a year. Under Hadley, the magazine's circulation increased tremendously.

Hadley recalled that one of her first duties was to conduct a readership survey, which had not been done before. Among the topics which readers showed significant interest in was historical stories. "I wasn't concentrating on history, but when you're doing a state magazine, you have to look at the state's past and present," she said. "We always tried to do a history piece or two in every issue."

Hadley said her goal with *Nevada Magazine* was to "show the soul of the state." During her tenure, the magazine became a lively mixture of features and photos spotlighting the excitement of Las Vegas and Reno as well as the state's history, culture, and beauty. "In particular, I wanted to turn on the Californians to come and spend their money here," she says.

In 1985, Hadley departed to pursue other projects—today she rides herd on *Range Magazine*—and was followed by Kirk

Whisler, former publisher of *Caminos* magazine in Los Angeles. During Whisler's seven-year tenure the magazine became self-supporting and was produced by desktop publishing. Additionally, Whisler introduced the popular Nevada Events section.

Nevada Magazine has clearly changed since the days when Fred Greulich would, as Atwater recalled, sit in a chair at the state printing office and doze while he waited for copies to roll off the presses. Today, the magazine has full color photos, stories about casinos, and advertising. But in important ways, *Nevada Magazine* hasn't changed. The stories and photos still highlight the state's history, culture, and landscape. And, occasionally, those wonderful roads are mentioned.

—Richard Moreno

MORNIN' ON THE DESERT

(Originally appeared in March 1936)

Mornin' on the desert, and the wind is blowin' free,
And it's ours, jest for the breathin', so let's fill up, you and me.
No more stuffy cities, where you have to pay to breathe,
Where the helpless human creatures move and throng and
   strive and seethe.

Mornin' on the desert, and the air is like a wine,
And it seems like all creation has been made for me and mine.
No house to stop my vision, save a neighbor's miles away,
And the little dobe shanty that belongs to me and May.

Lonesome? Not a minute! Why I've got these mountains here,
That was put here jest to please me, with their blush and frown
   and cheer.
They're waitin' when the summer sun gets too sizzlin' hot,
An' we jest go campin' in 'em with a pan an' coffee pot.

Mornin' on the desert—I can smell the sagebrush smoke,
I hate to see it burnin', but the land must sure be broke.
Ain't it jest a pity that wherever man may live,
He tears up much that's beautiful that the good God has to give?

Sagebrush ain't so pretty? Well, all eyes don't see the same.
Have you ever saw the moonlight turn it to a silvery flame?
An' that greasewood thicket yonder—well, it smells jest awful sweet.

When the night wind has been shakin' it—for its smell is hard
   to beat.
Lonesome? Well, I guess not! I've been lonesome in a town.
But I sure do love the desert with its stretches wide and brown.
All day through the sagebrush here the wind is blowin' free,
An' it's ours jest for the breathin', so let's fill up, you and me.

Found written on the door of an old cabin in Southern Nevada.

PRINCES OF THE FOURTH ESTATE

Anyone who read the *Territorial Enterprise* of the early 1860s
could have told you which of its two local reporters would go on
to fame and fortune. Mark Twain? No, Dan De Quille.

(Originally appeared in Winter 1979)

By David W. Toll

The long lost *Territorial Enterprise* was one of the great news-papers on the frontier West. So brilliant was its history that books have been written about it, and in one of them, *Comstock Commotion,* Lucius Beebe writes: "The story of the *Enterprise* in its early years is a story of perfect timing. Almost at the very moment that Goodman and McCarthy assumed com-plete ownership, it became established that the Comstock's surface diggings and ores of easily accessible outcrop-pings were actually the merest superficial traces of incalculable bonanzas which would be available for deep mining."

The timing, of course was perfect but what made the *Enterprise* a great paper was its staff, and the roster of names reads like a Murderer's Row of frontier Western journalists.

Mark Twain

PHOTO: BANCROFT LIBRARY

Editor Joe Goodman had been the founder of the *Golden Era,* a popular monthly published in San Francisco during the tumultuous years of the California gold rush. He was a practical printer, a poet of high reputation, and an accomplished duelist as he demonstrated in 1863 by shooting Tom Fitch in the knee. Fitch was the editor of the *Virginia City Union.*

Goodman's partner, Denis McCarthy, ran the mechanical

side of the paper and later published the *Virginia Evening Chronicle* for many years.

Rollin Daggett, later Congressman, and after that United States Minister to King Kalakaua of Hawaii, was Goodman's associate editor and himself a celebrated writer. "The pen, in his hand, is like a mighty trip-hammer, which is so nicely adjusted he can, at will, strike a blow which seems like a caress, and the next moment hurl hundred-ton blows, one after another, with the quickness of lightning, and filling all the air around with fire." That was the assessment of Judge C.C. Goodwin, himself an *Enterprise* editor in the 1870s who later edited the *Salt Lake City Tribune* for more than 20 years.

And as local reporters, Mark Twain and Dan De Quille.

Dan De Quille—born William Wright in Iowa in 1829—had come west in 1857, leaving his wife and daughter behind in West Liberty, Iowa, as he tried his luck in the California gold fields. While working as a miner, he also wrote articles and sketches for magazines including the *Golden Era*. He came to the Comstock in 1860, settling in Silver City as a prospector, and when Joe Goodman and Denis McCarthy took over the *Enterprise* in 1861 he began sending them correspondence. He was hired as local reporter that year, and by the time Sam Clemens joined the staff in the spring of 1862, Dan De Quille was already acquiring a reputation for his graceful and elaborate hoaxes, like the "Traveling Stones of the Pahranagat Valley," which inspired offers from P.T. Barnum and scholarly inquiries from Europe, and for his detailed and cogent reporting on the mines.

"In those early days there were in the town many desperate characters," De Quille later wrote, "and bloody affrays were of

Dan De Quille

PHOTO: NEVADA HISTORICAL SOCIETY

frequent occurrence. Sometimes while a reporter was engaged in gleaning the particulars in regard to some shooting scrape another would start (growing out of something said in regard to the first), and the news gatherer suddenly found himself in the midst of flying bullets, and had before him a battle, the particulars in regard to which he need not take at second hand."

De Quille also recalled that in those early days "the arrival of an emigrant train was still a big event. The 'captain' and other leading men of the train were concerned and encouraged to relate all of interest that had happened during the journey across the plains. The train often remained encamped in the suburbs of town several days before proceeding to California, and before they left, all hands were pretty thoroughly 'pumped.'"

When Mark Twain joined the growing *Enterprise* staff he was a careless, abrasive Missourian who took a reporter's job because he preferred using a pencil to a shovel. Until February 1863, he signed himself Josh and sent in correspondence from Aurora before being offered the $25-a-week job.

"I can never forget my first day's experience as a reporter," he wrote 10 years later in *Roughing It*. Among other hilarious and dumbfounding experiences he recalled that he had found some emigrant wagons going in to camp and had learned "that they had lately come through hostile Indian country and had fared rather roughly. I made the best of the item that the circumstances permitted, and felt that if I were not confined within the rigid limits by the presence of the reporters of the other papers I could add particulars that would make the article that much more interesting. However, I found one wagon that was going to California, and made some judicious inquiries of the proprietor. When I learned, through his short and surly answers to my cross-questioning, that he was certainly going on and would not be in the city the next day to make trouble, I got ahead of the other papers, for

I took down his list of names and added his party to the killed and wounded. Having more scope here, I put this wagon through an Indian fight that to this day has no parallel in history.

"My two columns were filled. When I read them over in the morning I felt that I had found my legitimate vocation at last. I reasoned with myself that news, and stirring news too, was what a paper needed, and I felt I was particularly endowed with the ability to furnish it. Mr. Goodman said that I was as good a reporter as Dan. I desired no higher commendation. With encouragement like that, I felt I could take my pen and murder all the emigrants on the plains if need be and the interests of the paper demanded it."

Those two quick glimpses of the wagon trail are enough to hint at the characteristic differences in viewpoint of the reporters: De Quille's clear, straightforward description versus Twain's distorted and exaggerated vision.

It is easy to picture them as they sat on a winter's night at a table in the press room, stabbing their steel-nibbed pens into a shared ink bottle, scribbling madly and bantering back and forth: 27-year-old Mark Twain, stocky and rumpled, with a bushy auburn mustache and the eyes of a wolf. Dan De Quille, 33, tall, slender, and dark, a stringy black beard and an amiable nature. As it is completed, each story is handed to the printers, whose hands fly over the type cases like trained birds, and the reporters drink beer while they wait for the proofs, each reading the other's copy. Twain remarks that it is cold out, and De Quille launches into an animated description of the former *Enterprise* building on A Street, with its simultaneous extremes of hot and cold when the stove was stoked up until it glowed cherry red in the freezing building. Everyone pulled their writing tables and type cases as close to the stove as they could get, and the pressmen worked with their feet wrapped in burlap bags against the biting cold.

But that wasn't the worst of it. The worst of it was when the weather warmed up a little and all the snow and ice began to melt and trickle through the holes in the roof. He pantomimed for the grinning Twain how they had tacked strings to the ceiling at the worst of leaks, to lead the dripping water over to the side of the structure away from the furniture and machinery. Sometimes there were so many, he said, that the upper part of the building looked as if it were festooned with cobwebs, the gleaming wet webs of some hideous huge spider.

When they had corrected the proofs, they shouldered their way into heavy wool coats and thundered down the stairs to the wooden sidewalk of C Street, and hurried south through the frosty night to the International Bar, where they swept in almost to applause, minor princes of the fourth estate, to drink whiskey and eat oysters in the company of prosperous men.

From the International they pushed out into the frozen night again and climbed Union Street to their B Street boardinghouse. There Mark stealthily helped himself to a wedge of the mince pie left out to cool in the kitchen and to four or five sticks of firewood from Tom Fitch's wood box to heat the room he shared with Dan. Some nights they didn't go home at all but trooped up and down the streets until dawn, sometimes with an excursion to the D Street line. Other nights they stayed on at the office, writing until breakfast, through the clatter of the thrashing presses and the chattering of the newsboys coming in at six. Mark Twain and Dan De Quille partnered for more than a year as reporters on the *Enterprise,* and years later Joe Goodman remarked that if anyone had asked him at the time which of the two would emerge as a leading American literary figure, he would have answered without hesitation: Dan De Quille.

Well, we all know how that worked out. Twenty years later Mark Twain was spending his mornings in bed, propped up on silken pillows and smoking cigars the size of dynamite sticks, writing his immensely popular books, making huge investment blunders, and vacationing in Bermuda. Dan De Quille was still pondering the board sidewalks of Virginia City, drawing his $50 a week and gathering news for the *Enterprise.*

Until the late 1800s he was a familiar sight limping along the shabby streets of the played out city in his antiquated black cloak and his sparse chin whiskers, an eccentric old mandarin.

Alf Doten, himself a daily reporter for the *Union* and later for the *Enterprise* before becoming editor and publisher of the *Gold Hill News,* kept a daily journal all his life. Dan De Quille's name appears in it often during the 1860s, most frequently in connection with the late nights and drinking sprees. On Christmas Eve 1869, Doten noted in his journal, "Ran the *News* till we got it to press, then walked to Virginia and this evening ran the *Enterprise,* as Dan is discharged again for drunkenness."

De Quille was rehired, and served the *Enterprise* more or less faithfully until 1885, when he was let go. He was employed again in 1887, and Doten's journals again mentioned his former colleague of earlier years. April 14, 1887: "Dan De Quille got drunk again today for the first time since he has been back in his old position as local of the *Enterprise.*" June 23, 1887: "About 7 PM met Taggart on the street and he got me to fix up the local department of the *Enterprise,* Dan being to drunk—he has been drinking heavily for the last few days & other parties have had to do his work occasionally." June 27: "Was about getting items, but Dan was sober enough to work tonight, so I was not needed."

June 29, 1888: "Dan on deck again." Eventually Dan's career evaporated, and he got by on a small pension paid by a mining magnate John Mackay.

On July 14, 1897, after nearly 40 years on the Comstock,

Alf Doten

PHOTO: NEVADA HISTORICAL SOCIETY

Dan De Quille went east to die. The following entry is in Alf Doten's journal for that date. "On board the passenger train this afternoon I found Dan De Quille (William Wright), wife and daughter Lou—I had a talk with Dan during the ten minute stop—Going to West Liberty, Iowa, their old home . . . He never expects to come back, for he is so terribly broken down with rheumatism and used up generally that he cannot live long anyway—Is racked with it from shoulders to knees, back humped up double and is merely animated skin and bone, almost helpless—can only walk about the house a little, grasping cane with both hands—has not been able to walk down from his residence on A St., Va., to C St. and back for nearly or quite two years—looks to be 90 years old, yet was 68 on 9th of May last—2 months and 10 days older than I am— Promised to write me when he gets home—Poor old dear boy Dan—my most genial companion in our early Comstock reportorial days, good-bye, and I think forever personally on this earth . . . "

Dan De Quille died March 16th, 1898, and comparisons with his old partner are irresistible: spectacular Twain the grand success and quiet De Quille the seedy failure.

But that is not the way they were remembered in Virginia City. Joe Farnsworth, the former state printer, now deceased, gave his youth to the *Enterprise* back shop in the 1890s and learned about Twain from the old timers who had known him in the early days. "From them I gathered the impression that Clemens was regarded as the prime s.o.b. of Virginia City while he was here." Farnsworth heard Twain damned as a foul-minded, dirty talking four flusher.

"One old fellow used a phrase I remember: 'Mark Twain had no earmuffs on when somebody was buying. He could hear a live one order a round three doors from where he was standing. But he was deaf as a post when it was his turn to shout.'

"I never heard admiration expressed for him personally by

men who knew him personally," Farnsworth said. "Everybody on staff hated Mark Twain and everybody really loved Dan De Quille. I think he was the most wonderful old man I ever knew. He couldn't say three words to you before you were friends for life and wanted to put your arms around him.

"At the time I speak of he was poor as a church mouse. I don't know what he did with his money, but in his old age I know he didn't drink at all ... He was the grand old man of Virginia City and everyone in Nevada knew him by sight. I never knew a man more loved and respected."

Judge C.C. Goodwin wrote the obituary of Dan that took more than a column on the front page of the *Enterprise*. In it he coined the phrase that ought to be carved on Dan's tombstone: "He was the most efficient and valuable man that ever wore out his life in a newspaper office."

NEVADA'S FIRST WOMAN SHERIFF

In 1919 Clara Dunham Crowell was the law in Lander County.
(Originally appeared in January/February 1981)

By Craig MacDonald

It was evening when the stage came rolling up to the Two Bit House in Austin, Nevada. Teamster George Crowell climbed down from the box. Crowel was eager to fill his empty stomach with a warm meal, but he was even more anxious to chat with an amiable waitress who always showed an interest in his arrival.

Clara Dunham was able to put George at ease and take his mind off the rigors of the road. And certainly George was impressed with the attentive lady from Austin, enough so that he started seeing more of her, and they were married in 1898.

The Crowell family flourished. The couple had two children, and George, who was highly regarded for his honesty and "can do" attitude, was elected sheriff of Lander County.

He tackled the job with the same enthusiasm he used to drive his old six-horse stage. Clara learned much from her husband about the qualities of a good sheriff—how to anticipate trouble, how to keep calm, and how to use a gun.

George and Clara Crowell

Clara herself was not in the habit of running from trouble. During his stage-driving days George often returned late from Goldfield or Tonopah, and if he was carrying company money, he would keep it safe at home until the bank opened the next morning. One night Clara and her niece Ruth were in the house—George had been called out—when a strange man knocked on the door. "I know there's money in there," he said. "Open up or you'll be sorry."

Clara opened the door in his face and demanded, "What will I be sorry for?" Then she chased him out the gate.

As sheriff George Crowell did his job well and was highly respected for maintaining peace in the sometimes volatile county of Lander. But he was struck down by illness, and in February 1919, while he was trying to recuperate in the milder climate of Oakland, California, George Crowell died. The people of Lander were shocked by the news. But it did not take them long to decide who should take George's place.

Local men and women circulated a petition calling for Clara Dunham Crowell to become the first woman sheriff in Nevada history.

The *Reese River Reveille* reported, "There were several male aspirants for the job but none made a formal application after the petition was circulated and presented to the county commissioners." Upon seeing the petition, the commissioners unanimously selected 42-year-old Clara Crowell to be sheriff for the remaining two years of her husband's term.

On March 8, 1919, the *Battle Mountain Scout* declared, "The county is unique in its appointment of a woman as sheriff. Being a woman does not in any way interfere with the performance of duty and there is no doubt in the minds of the people that duty will be the watchword of Mrs. Crowell.

"If she needs any help from the outside, there are plenty of men who are ready and willing to do the rough part of the work for her."

But Clara proved that she could handle any situation. She was involved in the apprehension of cattle rustlers, horse thieves, robbers, and other criminals. As sheriff she demanded respect for the law in Lander. She and her deputy, Thomas

White, even enforced the new Dry Law, which among other things prevented people from transporting bottles of liquor. "The Dry Law has been looked upon as more or less of a joke," report the *Reveille*. "The officers are making a drive to show that the law, be it good or bad, must be respected."

Sheriff Crowell proved to be a woman of action. She collared some crooks by working undercover. Once she posed as an old Indian to catch a man who was selling liquor illegally to Indians. After catching the storekeeper in the act, Clara threw open her coat, exposing the sheriff's badge, and placed the man under arrest.

Once Clara went into the mountains and brought back a man suspected of fraud, and the *Reveille* ran the following page one headline: "Lady Sheriff Brings Back Her Prisoner." The reporter noted, "Her friends were somewhat surprised that she went after the prisoner herself instead of sending a deputy."

On several occasions she even entered saloons and broke up brawls. In an administrative overhaul, she removed Deputy White, who had served under four sheriffs. Clara Dunham Crowell earned a reputation throughout the West as a tough law officer.

When Clara's term came to an end many people encouraged her to run for election. But she was respected also for her nursing skills, and she decided to take the job of matron, or administrator, of the county hospital, a position she held for the next 20 years.

And, when she died at age 66 on June 19, 1942, it was only fitting that a grand tribute was made in Austin by the people Clara and George Crowell had served so faithfully. The populace packed the flower-laden Masonic Odd Fellows Hall for the services, and District Attorney Howard Browne delivered a stirring eulogy, tracing the remarkable career of the waitress who left the Two Bit House to become the first woman sheriff in Nevada.

BUTCH CASSIDY AND THE GREAT WINNEMUCCA BANK ROBBERY

On that day in 1900 the famous outlaw rode out of town in a hail of bullets.
Or did he?

(Originally appeared in May/June 1983)

By David W. Toll

Butch Cassidy (right) and the Hole in the Wall Gang.

Winnemucca is a tranquil town on the Humboldt River, a trading post transformed by the railroad into a lively shipping center, a bumptious cow town and county seat. Its history resembles that of dozens of other Western railroad towns, except for one transcendent event:

On September 19, 1900, as the story goes, Butch Cassidy rode into Winnemucca and robbed the local bank.

Butch and the boys got clean away, galloping out of town in

a hail of bullets, with $32,000 in gold. Later on, the story tells us, he added insult to injury by sending the bank a photograph of himself and the boys in fancy new suits, stiff collars, and derbies. With it was a mocking thank-you note expressing appreciation for the Winnemucca money they were using to pay for their fun.

It is a delicious story, and it has been told and retold countless times. I have told it myself. It is such a wonderful story that the community long celebrated Butch Cassidy Days every September in honor of the great event.

But unfortunately it is not a true story. In fact, Butch Cassidy never sent that picture, and the evidence is pretty clear that he was never in Winnemucca in his life.

The great robbery did take place, all right. It may be that Butch Cassidy knew the robbery was going to happen. He might even have had a hand in making the arrangements, although that was never proved. It is also possible that some of his larcenous friends in the Wild Bunch were involved. But no matter who robbed the Winnemucca bank, no one who was there that day would ever forget it.

THE BOYS

Winnemucca, 1900. Like a new mother gazing down at her sleeping babe, the September sun lavished light and warmth on the dusty burg at the big bend of the Humboldt. The town was busy with stockmen buying and selling cattle and horses when sharply at noon the schoolhouse doors burst open, and the pent-up kids came streaming out and down the steps and home for lunch.

Some of the boys liked to walk down Bridge Street to the river and chunk rocks into the shallow water until it was time to go back to class. So it was that nine-year-old Lee Case and a couple of his pals were on their way back from the river one day when they trooped past the empty livery stable and saw some cowboys sitting by the open doorway. In their friendly way the cowboys struck up a conversation with the boys. The next day they saw the men there again, and talked with them some more. They were just drifting cowboys passing through, making small talk about the town, asking how many deputies there were, and one thing and another.

George Nixon

PHOTO: NEVADA HISTORICAL SOCIETY

East of town about 10 miles, another boy got to know the three cowboys. Ten-year-old Vic Button rode to Golconda to school every day, passing their camp in a hayfield down near the river where there was a well for drinking water. There was nothing out of the ordinary about that. The roundups were about over, and plenty of cowboys were moving throughout the country. Vic would have ridden right on by the men's camp except for the handsome white horse that caught his eye.

Vic rode over and asked the cowboy if he'd like to trade his white horse. The cowboy laughed and said no, he'd keep him a while. But Vic had fallen in love with that big white horse. The next day at his father's ranch, the CS, he picked out a fine strong saddle horse and rode it to the camp in hopes of a trade, but it was no dice. The cowboys were friendly, and jawed with the kid, and wondered out loud what the best way might be to get to southern Idaho in a hurry from there, and they nodded their heads when Vic pointed out Soldier Pass.

Vic rode a different horse past the camp to school each day, hoping one of them would take the cowboy's eye the way the white had taken his. But the cowboy wouldn't trade.

THE HOLDUP

September 19 was another golden day, and at noon the schoolboys hurried home for lunch as usual. Carl Smith took his customary walk down to the corner of Fourth

Street and then turned and walked along the sidewalk next to the First National Bank. As usual, he looked in the window as he went by.

But most unusually he saw Mr. McBride, Mr. Calhoun, and Mr. Hill standing by their desks behind the counter with their hands up in the air. Two men were pointing long-barreled pistols at their frightened faces. Over by the big safe a man with a scraggy yellow beard had ahold of Mr. Nixon with one hand and held a great, gleaming knife at his throat with the other.

Carl walked directly home as usual, ate his lunch in silence, and went back to school by the long way, so completely flummoxed by what he had seen that he didn't say a word about it to anyone until it was all over.

Lee Case and Slats Rutherford, meanwhile, were walking past the courthouse when they heard a burst of loud popping and stopped in wonder at the sound.

What they heard was banker George Nixon shooting his six-gun in the air in the street outside the bank. Nixon had opened the safe with that knife at his throat and watched helplessly as the bearded man had reached inside and thrust three bags full of gold coins into an ore sack he had brought along. Afterwards he had emptied the money drawer in Nixon's private office of the 10- and 20-dollar gold coins kept there.

Then everyone had been herded into the bank's small backyard—Nixon, his three employees, and W. S. Johnson, a horse-buyer who had been in Nixon's office when the robbers arrived. While the bearded man held them at gunpoint, the other two robbers had jumped the back fence and run down the alley to their tethered horses. When the man with the blond beard had gone over the fence after them, Nixon led the rush back into the bank. Grabbing up his hidden revolver, Nixon ran into the street to give the alarm. Johnson, the horsebuyer, meanwhile snatched a "pumping gun" off the wall, ran back into the yard and over the fence, and drew down on the robbers as they sped away on horseback.

But—click—the gun was empty.

Deputy Sheriff George Rose then ran out of the courthouse with a rifle in his hand. He raced past Lee and Slats and climbed a windmill that gave him a view over the slaughter-house roof. Another spatter of popping broke out, and the boys followed him up the tower in time to see that the robbers were having a little trouble getting out of town.

Galloping down Second Street, one of them had seen Sheriff Charles McDeid standing outside the Reception Saloon and sent him ducking back inside with pistol shot. They had taken the corner at Cross's Creek full tilt, and in the process the money bag had slipped loose and fallen to the street, scattering coins. The robbers hauled up their horses, wheeled, and plunged back to where the sack lay in the street. One of the men dismounted and handed the bag back up to a second man, while the third was attending to the pursuit with his six-gun.

Back at the bank, Johnson threw down his pumping gun in the alley in disgust, and after George Nixon emptied his gun in the air, Calhoun, the stenographer, followed the robbers on foot. As Golconda's newspaper, the *Silver State*, explained the next day, he "accidentally turned the corner where the men had dropped that sack and one of the robbers good-natured-ly took three shots at Mr. Calhoun, who promptly fell behind a fence."

As Calhoun tumbled out of sight and the robber leapt back into the saddle, the door of the cottage behind the bandits opened. Chris Lane poked his head out and angrily began lecturing the horsemen about shooting off their guns inside the town limits. A bullet splintered the door frame over Lane's head, and he jumped back inside. The three men spurred their horses and dashed away, leaving gold coins glittering in the dirt where the bag had fallen.

THE CHASE

While their pursuers scratched in the street for coins, the bandits raced out of town on the Golconda Road. Seeing them go, Deputy Rose climbed down the windmill, hurried to a nearby railroad spur, and commandeered a switch engine and its crew to chase the rapidly departing bad men. When Lee and Slats climbed on, Deputy Rose ordered the kids off, and they had to jump down, but as soon as the deputy turned his back, Slats scrambled back on board.

The robbers had a good lead on the engine, and at the Sloan Ranch, about eight miles out of town, they changed over to fresh horses. In the process they took three fine saddle horses belonging to George Nixon, including his personal favorite. They galloped on, with the little switch engine slowly gaining. Deputy Rose was poised at its nose, waiting to get within rifle range, and Slats Rutherford had his head down and his heart in this throat, hanging on at the back of the engine.

About 11 miles out of town Deputy Rose began lobbing shots at the fleeing robbers, and the *Silver State* the next day gave him credit for wounding one of Nixon's horses. Nevertheless, the barbed-wire fence that had kept the horsemen penned beside the tracks had been cut, and they sprinted north out of rifle range to another change of horses near their little camp by the river. There they transferred the gold to a packhorse and rode away.

Posses were formed, trackers put on the trail, and telegrams sent to law officers in the surrounding districts. The chase was on. If the men dispatched from Golconda had taken a slightly different route, they'd have cut the trail ahead of the robbers; as it was they caught up to them where they were changing horses at Clover Valley, on the way to Soldier Pass. The posse couldn't keep up with the fresh horses, but it did get close enough that one of the bandits stood up in the saddle and yelled back at them: "Give the white horse to the kid on the CS Ranch!"

They did, and for years afterward Vic Button rode his white horse, Patsy, all around that country.

The progress of the chase from Wednesday, September 19, to Thursday September 27, is told in the headlines of the *Silver State*.

FIRST NATIONAL BANK ROBBED
Three Desperadoes Loot It and Secure Thousands of Dollars.

Cashier and Assistants Forced to Hand Over the Money to the Robbers, Who Afterward Escape with Their Booty.

ROBBERS ARE HARD PRESSED
Last Reports Say Posse Was Not Far Behind.

Desperadoes Are Heading for the Junipers Country—News of a Fight Is Expected Hourly.

CHASE OF THE ROBBERS
Were Near Tuscarora Last Night.

STRONG POSSE
IS PURSUING THEM
Last News Received Indicates the Capture of Desperadoes.

ROBBERS STILL AT LARGE
Posses Still After Them But There Is No News of the Chase.

THE ROBBER HUNT
Posse Still Following Them Through Wilds of Northern Idaho

NO FURTHER NEWS OF ROBBERS

DUVIVIER RETURNS
At Last Accounts Posse Was Far Behind Robbers.

LOST TRAIL OF ROBBERS
Only Chance of Capture Now Is by Posse From Idaho.

After that, nothing. The robbers had disappeared.

THE EVIDENCE

There was no lack of suspects. Even before the dust of the chase settled, the *Silver State* printed a long roster of candidates. In describing the tail end of the chase a week after the robbery, the *Silver State* mentioned that "two hard characters from Wyoming who had been around White Rock for some time are also believed to be connected with the robbery."

George Nixon pressed a vigorous investigation. He hired Tom Horn, the notorious enforcer of the Wyoming Cattlemen's Association, and paid numerous informants. In correspondence with the Pinkerton Detective Agency, Nixon guaranteed payment of $1,000 for each of the robbers, dead or alive, and said he would also commit one-fourth of the recovered loot, and even more if there were significant risk or expense involved.

About six weeks after the robbery someone got around to searching the campsite near the river and found the torn-up scraps of three letters, which Nixon himself taped back together to send to the Pinkertons.

One of the letters, postmarked September 1, 1900, at Riverside, Wyoming, was addressed to C. E. Rowe, Golconda, Nevada. "Dear Friend," it said. "Yours at hand this evening. We are glad to know you are getting along well. In regards to sale enclosed letter will explain everything. I am so glad that everything is favorable. We have left Baggs, so write us at Encampment, Wyoming. Hoping to hear from you soon I am as ever, your friend Mike."

Another letter was written on blue paper with the letterhead of attorney D. A. Pristine of Rock Springs, Wyoming. It was dated August 24, 1900, and read, "My Dear Sir, Several influential parties are becoming interested and the chances of a sale are becoming favorable. Yours, Truly, D. A. Preston."

The third letter was written in the same handwriting as the second, and on the same blue paper, but with no letterhead and no salutation. "Send me a map of the country," it said, "and describe as near as you can the place where you found the black stuff so I can go to it. Tell me how you want it handled. You don't know its value. If I can get hold of it first, I can fix a good many things favorable. Say nothing to anyone about it." It was signed simply, "P."

Douglas A. Preston was Butch Cassidy's lawyer and had represented other members of the Wild Bunch in their scrapes with the law.

There were other hints of a Wyoming connection. One of the getaway horses wore a Wyoming brand and was discovered to have been rustled. There were those "two hard characters from Wyoming," who reportedly met the robbers in the wilderness of southeastern Idaho and disappeared with them.

THE PHOTOGRAPH

A few years ago, two bound volumes of letters were found in the basement of the old bank building. They turned out to be copies of George Nixon's business correspondence from February 24, 1900, to October 9, 1905. The letters were later given to Lee Berk, a longtime Winnemucca resident and ardent student of its history. In turn, Mr. Berk passed them on to the Nevada Historical Society. The letters shed light on a number of important events of the time, and 28 of them are devoted to various aspects of the robbery.

One interesting aspect of the letters is that nowhere is there any suggestion that the famous photograph, or any note or other communications, had been received from the bandits. Mr. Berk has read every issue of the *Silver State* for years after the robbery, and nowhere has he found a reference to the famous photograph or the mocking note.

In fact, it was the Pinkertons who sent George Nixon the photograph—more than five months after the robbery took place.

The photograph was discovered by a Wells Fargo detective

working undercover as a gambler in Fort Worth, Texas, to track down the survivors of the Black Jack Ketchum gang. The detective was strolling down Main Street one day when he happened to pass the Swartz photography studio and noticed a picture on display of five dapper dudes in their new threads. He was startled and pleased to recognize the handsome young man standing on the left as Bill Carver, one of the men he was searching for. The others were quickly identified as Harvey Logan (Kid Curry); Harry Longabaugh (alias Harry Alonzo, alias the Sundance Kid); Ben Kilpatrick (alias the Tall Texan), another one of the Ketchum bunch; and Butch Cassidy.

Wells Fargo sent a copy of the photograph to the Pinkertons, who were investigating the Winnemucca robbery on behalf of the American Bankers Association. They sent it, along with some mug shots, to George Nixon in Winnemucca for his identification.

"While I am satisfied that Cassidy was interested in the robbery," Nixon wrote in reply on January 8, 1901, "he was not one of the men who entered the bank."

A month and a half later, however, Nixon conceded, "So far as Cassidy is concerned we will be willing to take chances in paying the reward for him upon the evidence now in hand." But he emphasized that Cassidy had not been one of the robbers. "I am trying to get a description of Cassidy from a person who formerly knew him, as the photograph you sent me is the likeness of a man with a great deal squarer cut face and massive jaws, in fact somewhat of a bulldog appearance, while the man 'Whiskers' struck me as a face that, in case it was shaven, would have more of a coyote appearance."

A quick look at the famous photograph show four strong chins. Only Harvey Logan looks like a coyote, and Nixon tentatively identified him as one of the other men. "After studying the photo of Harvey Logan, which you sent me, both Mr. McBride and myself are of the opinion that he is #2," he wrote. As for robber #3, Nixon added with obvious hesitation,

"I am also about confident now that he was Harry Alonzo."

It seems scarcely a firm identification, but on May 15, 1901, the Pinkerton Detective Agency offered a $6,000 reward for the arrest of the Winnemucca robbers. The flyer contained descriptions of the three men who had entered the bank, and stated:

"After a thorough investigation, and from information received, George Parker (right name) alias George Cassidy, alias "Butch" Cassidy, alias Ingerfield; and Harry Longbaugh [sic] alias 'Kid' Longbaugh, alias Harry Alonzo, are suspected of being two of the men engaged in this robbery."

THE VERDICT

While the flyer was being distributed to law officers around the country, Butch, Sundance, and Etta Place were in New York, enjoying a farewell round of parties and pleasures before sailing to Buenos Aires and a new series of adventures in South America.

A Pinkerton detective eventually tracked them to Argentina, but he didn't pursue them into the interior, where they were ranching at Cholila in Chubut province. When Butch and Sundance were reported killed by soldiers of the Bolivian Army a few years later, the Pinkertons closed their files on them. No one was ever arrested for robbing the Winnemucca bank, and the reward was never paid.

This much we know: Butch Cassidy wasn't there, and he didn't send that photograph either.

The rest is theory, but there is plenty of that. Lee Berk has come to believe that some local person—C.E. Rowe, perhaps, or one of the suspects listed in the paper, or someone whose name never came to light—recognized the bank as a plum ripe for the picking and got word to the Wild Bunch in Wyoming. Then some of the boys rode in to look the situation over and later did the job. At 91, Lee Case can plainly remember his shock and surprise at seeing his cowboy friends from the livery stable stampeding out of town in a blaze of gunfire, but he can't recall that they ever mentioned their names.

Another persistent theory says that the robbery was an inside job, and that George Nixon had conspired to rob his own bank. One variant of this theory has the horsebuyer Johnson actually being Butch Cassidy himself. But Johnson was a real person, well known and well documented. An impersonation is out of the question.

Another version of the inside-job theory has George Wingfield as mastermind. Wingfield, later a mining millionaire and political boss of Nevada, had appeared in Tonopah not long after the robbery with a grubstake provided by Nixon. He and Nixon were partners in numerous enterprises, including great bonanza mines at Goldfield and a chain of banks. It is perhaps tempting to picture them scheming to fake the robbery.

But Wingfield was already a well-known character in the region, having run a saloon in Golconda and raised horses on a ranch nearby. His comings and goings were noted in the newpaper. He could never have taken an active part in the robbery without being recognized.

And George Nixon didn't need to fake any holdup. He was doing very well on the square, as he did all his life, becoming very rich from his Goldfield speculations, building a chain of banks and a mansion on the Truckee bluffs in Reno, and in 1905 ascending to the U.S. Senate. He was the very model of success, a paragon of rectitude, the hardworking hero of a Horatio Alger life.

I still miss Butch Cassidy Days. So instead, I'm going to camp on the doorstep of the fancy Nixon Mausoleum at Mountain View Cemetery in Reno. I want to listen to the rattle of the good banker's bones as he rolls over in his coffin while the home folks honor the thieves, whoever they were, who held a knife at his throat and stole all the Winnemucca money.

PETTICOAT PROSPECTORS

A woman in Nevada's gold camps had to work harder than men, and also had to prove she could sting like a rattler if the occasion demanded.

(Originally appeared in November/December 1983)

By Terri Sprenger-Farley

Tales of the Comstock Lode—the camaraderie, hard work, adventure, and sudden wealth—filled the fantasies of many children in the late 1800s, and the images appealed as much to young girls as to their brothers. And more than a handful of those girls, grown up, leapt at the chance to strike it rich in Nevada's mining boom at the turn of the century— no matter the cost.

Trading tea dresses and milky complexions for trousers and skin as tough as mule hide was the first part of exchange. A lady prospector also had to work harder and longer than her fellows. She paid higher wages to those who deigned to help her in spite of her sex. And she toted a pistol in her waistband to show she was no tenderfoot and could sting like a rattler if the occasion demanded.

Luckily, Lillian Malcom was no tenderfoot when she arrived in the Bullfrog mining district in 1905. Bullfrog was at its most primitive stage. Miners' homes were dugouts or tents, huts made of mud and manure blocks or flour barrel frames covered with rough feed sacking. Prospectors in this rude town were eager for diversion. When Lillian, pretty and fresh from the Klondike, told her stories in boardinghouses (which were usually tents) for the price of a beefsteak (which cost as much as a man could mine in a month), even the most skeptical allowed that this little lady might make it.

Lillian had lived in a world of snow, dog sleds, and gold for several years. But the adventure which drove her to Nevada had been a spring snowshoe trek of 175 miles from Kugarrock

Alice "Happy Days" Diminy prospected in the Goldfield area.

to Nome in Alaska. "The ice was treacherous and the snow was melting," Lillian told listeners who sat on bedrolls or in the dirt. "The rivers were breaking up and we had to jump from one cake of ice to another. Once I fell in and nearly drowned.

"The party ran out of grub, and if it hadn't been for the tomakius—a short white pheasant—we would have been starved."

Miners weren't the only ones enthralled by Lillian's stories. Her looks and lively tongue made her an instant "character," and the newspapers loved her.

When Lillian announced that she and a couple of old timers were going to cross Death Valley looking for richer diggings, a crowd gathered in front of the Merchant Hotel to see her off, and the *Tonopah Bonanza* applauded her bravery in undertaking a trip "not always made without loss of life, even by strong, robust manhood.

"She did not betray any apprehension—on the contrary, she was smiling and happy and told reporters Death Valley had no terrors for her," the *Bonanza* marveled.

Then, because she was, after all, Bullfrog's leading lady, the newspaper described Lillian's "prospecting trousseau."

"Her hair was braided and tied in numerous labor-saving knots with white baby ribbons. Her face was pretty, but certain to lose its feminine delicacy and whiteness ere the sun's rays of Death Valley get through with it, especially as her light colored felt hat was narrow-brimmed."

Onlookers who appeared to be watching her four stamping horses might well have been considering her skirt length, which, the *Bonanza* reported, was quite a bit shorter than usual. It wasn't indecent, though, since it "Made a safe junction" with her tan boot tops.

Lillian said she had a pair of men's khakis in her saddlebags which she would don once she "got out a ways." Certainly it's only speculation that this remark enticed reporter Anthony MacCauley to accompany the prospecting troupe on its perilous journey.

While Lillian had to search for rich ground in California, two of her sister miners made themselves rich right in Goldfield. Mrs. Jennie Enright and Mrs. George H. Lewis were partners. They had bought their claim from another woman, Bessie Miller, who, according to the *Goldfield Daily Sun*, "parted with her holdings for a tidy sum," for they were still flushed with success from a $50,000 profit they'd made on another claim.

Their final transaction did involve a perilous journey, but it was more frightening for a San Francisco investor than for the veterans of Goldfield's petticoat brigade. L.R. Keough had come to see his company's interests. When he left with the two ladies on Saturday afternoon in August, intending to visit claims a few miles from town, he expected a pleasant outing. But the day grew dark and torrential rains destroyed their trail markers on the lake bed. It wasn't until 10 o'clock that night that Jennie, driving the skittish horses, spotted a landmark. They gathered ore samples and headed the team back toward Goldfield, where they arrived at 2 a.m. soaked and chilled.

"Mr. Keough was considerably impressed with the courage

of the women of the mining camps," the *Sun* bragged, "as well as their ability as horsewomen."

Keough was impressed enough that he set the women up with enough money to pursue their wildest prospecting dreams. The new Goldfield Gold Lake Mining Company brought Jennie and Mrs. George $5,000 in cash and 4,500 stock shares.

A dead man's map led Helen Cottrell to her fortune. She originally had to come to the Manhattan area to prospect, but things went sour, so Helen turned to the relatively safe and lucrative task of selling supplies to the miners she envied. But her dreams resurfaced when an exhausted prospector told her he was giving up.

His brother had mined the wilds of the Toiyabe Range before suddenly leaving for Mexico, where he had been killed by Yaqui Indians. Before his death he had drawn a detailed map of his claim and mailed it home. But, the prospector sighed, it hadn't led to any silver or even to the cabin his brother had described. He laughed at Helen's excitement and told her she was welcome to the useless scrap.

Helen's elation was contagious. She recruited two partners, and after a long search they found an old stone cabin and a forge with silver bits on it. The ore-rich ledge was harder to find, and the men with her almost gave up. Helen never did, although, she told reporters later, the place was so difficult to reach "a few more trips would have bankrupted me for clothing destroyed."

Helen's New Era Mine proved to contain gold and lead as well as silver. Unlike many Manhattan miners, she didn't sell out to San Francisco speculators who had invested heavily into the area, and that was just as well. Her discovery took place about the same time as the San Francisco earthquake of 1906. Bay Area investors pulled their money from Manhattan and put it into rebuilding San Francisco, leaving Manhattan's mines in the doldrums.

Helen's independent streak, typical of the petticoat prospectors, led her to even greater wealth on the Comstock. Not content to sit on her porch and watch ore cars roll to the smelter, Helen supervised some work she had commissioned in Gold Hill. She supervised very closely, and in 1907, clinging to the side of a 20-foot shaft, she recognized the little black threads of tellurium her workers had missed and withdrew an immediate $1,600 in gold.

Few women miners were as lucky at nabbing partners as Helen Cottrell. Their sex and independence were an unappealing combination to male adventurers of the time, so some women resorted to subterfuge to get desperately needed assistance.

The *Reno Evening Gazette* in 1908 reported one such attempt by an unnamed "hard-working woman" who had given up her attempts at recruiting local men. She skirted the issue of gender by hiring two miners through the mail.

Upon facing his lady boss, the experienced miner quit. But the other man smiled at the irony of his surprise. During their correspondence, he'd alluded to ore field experience he didn't have. He was a rank tenderfoot, as entranced with the lure of the rush as his employer. The two stuck together and surprised everyone by stumbling on a claim of gold-infused rock worth $4,000 per ton.

Happy Days Diminy was one of the hardest-working, longest-lived of the pioneering women. "No delicate, publicity-seeking effeminate imitation, but the genuine article," the *Goldfield Daily Tribune* called her. She was led to her first strike by ghosts.

Although her "sunny disposition, unchanged good nature, and smiling optimism" earned her nickname, Happy Days preferred to work alone. She had been doing so for five years when, in the summer of 1912, some folks said the solitude had scrambled her brain.

A dead woman friend appeared to Happy Days, flitting

about her land, snatching gold nuggets. Then a dream man materialized, explaining that the nuggets could be found here—he pointed—a mere 1,000 feet from her claim.

He was right. After many years of working the ground and hauling timber with only two burros for partners, Happy Days came to Goldfield with a bottle in her handbag. The bottle held a small collection of gold nuggets.

The sparseness of the discovery didn't seem to faze her. Like many of her female associates, Happy Days seemed to love the dream of wealth and the prospecting life as much as the gold itself.

The Goldfield that Happy Days knew was a town of contrasts. Inside the raucous saloons and dance halls, New York speculators in fine suits shared bar space with grizzled miners in sweat-stained khakis. Outside, the streets were jammed with businessmen from Chicago in their new Stanley cars, veering to miss braying, knee-locked burros. Goldfield had all the romantic excitement of the storied Comstock, and Happy Days swore she wouldn't miss it for the world. So, when she couldn't get San Francisco backing for her operation or even help from her husband, who had returned briefly from his own pursuits in Alaska, she pressed on alone.

She found a platinum deposit and bought herself a fruit ranch in California, and, for the first time, hired a young male helper to take a shovel to the 80-foot shaft she'd planned.

The young man, known as Smith, did his work well by all accounts. And if some folks made snide guesses about his true service to Happy Days, their speculation came to an end seven months into his employment.

"Woman Fighter Sends Man to Hospital," the *Tonopah Bonanza* blared. "Happy Days Called 'Some Scrapper.'" The newspaper reported Sheriff Ingalls had heard that Happy Days and Smith were engaged in a "rough and tumble scrap," which needed a lawman's intervention. But before he arrived, a man named Collitt had stepped in and helped the damsel in distress to "put the finishing touches" on Smith. Severe cuts, abrasions, and a broken arm sent Smith to the hospital, but Happy Days, whose injuries were comparable, balked at such treatment. As soon as she was placed on bond, she went home.

Physical injuries were just part of the territory. Unless they entailed copious amounts of blood, female miners were inclined to shrug them off.

A year before the fight Happy Days had received a concussion when her two burros, unused to harness, upset her wagon and ran over her. After dusting herself off, she was undoubtedly made an honorary member of Goldfield's "Tip-Over Club," which required being thrown from a car—a common occurrence in the early 1900s.

One of Happy Days' contemporaries fell down a 30-foot mine shaft and refused to leave her Goldfield cabin. Maggie Johnson, a black miner, was finally hospitalized over her protests because of crippling rheumatism. Elderly and ill, Maggie had been unable to work her claim for years but had lived on its earlier bounty, refusing to sell or lease her mine.

Happy Days was luckier. The *Ely Daily Times* reported that she was still going strong in 1942 at age 91. She was, in fact, demanding a divorce from her husband, 70-year-old H. Jester. Perhaps the marriage just couldn't stand the strain of Happy Days' spirit. Still seeking support for her mining efforts, Happy Days had ridden freight trains to New York to snare Wall Street backing. Her efforts had been futile, but she was undaunted.

Happy Days ended her life as many of her sister miners had prayed to end their own. She continued to live in the stone cabin she'd built by hand, continued to cultivate a garden each spring. And, hale and hardly in her jeans and jacket, Happy Days kept her prospector's dream alive long after it was a memory for the rest of Nevada, treading the path to Ely from her Tule Canyon claim, with a little bottle in her handbag, filled with flakes of gold.

QUEEN OF TARTS

Julia Bulette, the darling of Comstock folklore, has survived a century
of faded memories, historians' investigations, and her own murder.

(Originally appeared in September/October 1984)

By Susan James

efore climbing into bed on the evening of January 20,
1867, newspaperman Alf Doten, as always, recorded the
day's events in his diary. He wrote that singing, a turkey
dinner, and champagne had eased the bite of the Virginia City
winter, but an evening excursion had left him cold.
Doten and a friend had gone to view the
body of a woman "foully murdered in her
bed." He had little to say about the vic-
tim: "about 35 years old—prostitute."

In a few days, though, every resident
of the Comstock and half the West
knew that the woman's name was Julia
Bulette and that she had been the vic-
tim of what the *Territorial Enterprise*
called "the most cruel, outrageous, and
revolting murder ever committed in this
city." Prophetically, the *Virginia Daily
Union* stated, "Let a tear of sorrow for her
frailties take the place of scorn for her weak-
nesses, for she may yet bloom on the tree of immortality."

Such stories were to launch a legend. Her background and
violent death proved to be rich material for storytellers, and
Bulette in time found an impressive niche in Nevada's heritage. With the help of impassioned newspaper stories, dime
novels, and popular imagination, she became a legend, the
"Queen of the Red Lights," the darling of Comstock folklore.
Thanks to so much attention, by the middle of the 20th

Julia Bulette

PHOTO: NEVADA HISTORICAL SOCIETY

century Julia Bulette the frontier prostitute had been transformed into a stunning and affluent courtesan.

In fact, if "Jule" Bulette's friends read a modern biography of her, they would probably not recognize her. She was neither wealthy nor beautiful. She was little more than typical.

Julia and other prostitutes came to the Comstock in the early 1860s, keenly aware of how much money they could make in a mining town where the men outnumbered the women by nearly 40 to one. Journalists dubbed these camp followers "the fair, but frail." Respectable society shunned them, but prostitutes offered pleasure as well as companionship to the men who labored in the hellish abyss of the mines, enduring extremes of heat and cold as they dug the silver-rich ore from Mount Davidson. The delights of D Street's bawdy district gave them a chance to leave the inferno behind, if only for a while.

During her four years on the Comstock, Julia Bulette enjoyed moderate success. In the early morning hours of January 20, 1867, however, someone decided that Julia had more to offer than companionship. After a desperate struggle, the villain strangled her and fled unnoticed into the night with a booty of furs and jewels. The coroner's report said that she had sustained several heavy blows to the head before she died.

A friend and fellow prostitute, Gertrude Holmes, discovered Bulette's contorted body several hours later. Soon, Virginia City buzzed with the news of the crime. Local newspapers took advantage of the clamor by publishing sordid details of the death scene.

However, little was known about Bulette's background. According to the local newspapers, the young Englishwoman came to the Comstock in 1863 via New Orleans and the gold fields of California. The papers noted that somewhere along the way, Julia had married. The mysterious husband never appeared in Virginia City, where Bulette lived alone in a small rented cottage near the corner of D and Union streets.

Shortly after her arrival, Julia was elected an honorary member of Virginia City's Engine Company No 1. The title was apparently granted "in return for numerous favors and munificent gifts bestowed by her upon the company." The *Enterprise* called attention to Bulette's unflagging support of the fire department and her appearance at many fires where she was seen working the brakes of the engines. The company returned the favor by leading her funeral procession through the streets of the city. The weather was bad, though, and the firemen dropped out before the long, muddy trek to the Flowery Hill Cemetery east of town.

About 16 carriages filled with friends and members of the sisterhood accompanied Julia on her last journey. According to legend, the respectable ladies of the city quickly drew the curtain shades as the procession went by, no doubt hoping that their husbands were not among the mourners.

The Victorian society of the 19th century had mixed feelings about women whose choice of work led them into lives of disrepute. When given the opportunity, journalists and storytellers—the two differed little on the Comstock—seemed eager to romanticize them as fallen angels who could be paragons of virtue. Each candidate had to meet certain qualifications, though, and society was a fickle judge.

Julia Bulette had the essential prerequisites. First, so little was known about her life that her attributes could be greatly enhanced without fear of contradiction. More importantly, the combination of sex and violence captured the popular imagination at the time of Bulette's death, and journalists seized the opportunity to exploit the sensational nature of the murder. Finally, a public spectacle had to follow the murder and stir up the community's passions, as did the trial and hanging of Bulette's slayer.

Other candidates for legendhood, who probably deserved it more, did not fare as well because they lacked on the essential

John Millian

PHOTO: NEVADA HISTORICAL SOCIETY

themes. For example, two years before Bulette's murder, Virginia City madam Jessie Lester lost an arm from a gunshot wound. Tortured by pain, the unfortunate woman languished for nearly a month before she died from an infection in January of 1865, according to Alf Doten's diary. Jessie left most of her estate to the local Daughters of Charity for the care of orphans. The Catholic Church rewarded her generosity by burying her in consecrated ground. But philanthropy and a violent death weren't enough. She took the secret of her assailant's identity to her grave, thus depriving Virginia City residents of the opportunity to enjoy a lurid trial and a hanging. Jessie was soon forgotten.

When Julia Bulette died, the press wanted its readers to believe that the murderer had deprived the city of one of its most generous citizens. Bulette's only known contributions were to the local fire department. The *Union* also stated that she "possessed a benevolent disposition, her purse ever being open to the demands of charity, no matter what the form of application." Not wishing to be outdone by its competition, the *Territorial Enterprise* cited Bulette's "kind-hearted, liberal, benevolent and charitable disposition," adding that "few of her class had more true friends." The writer said that justice would only be served when authorities captured the despicable murderer and punished him for his deed.

Five months later, the press got its wish when officials took a destitute Frenchman, John Millian, into custody for the murder of Julia Bulette. After a well attended trial, a judge and jury convicted and sentenced him to hang. Once again, the *Enterprise* exaggerated Bulette's largesse when it noted that "hundreds in this city have had cause to bless her name for her many acts of kindness and charity," despite the fact that "she was a woman of easy virtue."

John Millian sat in jail for nearly a year, maintaining that two men had framed him for the murder, but authorities failed to locate them. On April 23, 1868, Millian ascended the gallows in front of about 4,000 spectators enjoying picnic lunches. Before the noose slid around his neck, the convicted murderer declared his innocence and thanked the ladies who had visited him in prison. (Despite the claims of the press, many of Virginia City's female residents were unwilling to acknowledge that Julia Bulette had made a significant contribution to the quality of life on the Comstock Lode.)

The hanging of John Millian brought an end to the sensation created by the murder of Julia Bulette, and interest in her story dwindled with the fortunes of the Comstock. The events of January 20, 1867, receded into the popular imagination until novelists resurrected them after Julia had lain in her grave for nearly 80 years.

The new biographers turned the 19th-century newspaper accounts to their advantage, adding grossly exaggerated details of the courtesan's life. The legend blossomed again as Julia received the attributes of royalty and a bank account to match. The woman the *Virginia Daily Union* describes as "comely" was now depicted as "elegant" and "warmly beautiful," her furs and jewelry the envy of every woman on the Comstock.

Writers speculated about Julia's ancestry. The fact that she might have lived in Louisiana was all they needed to transform the fair-skinned Englishwoman into a enticing New Orleans Creole. Exotic beauty was not among Julia's assets, but it didn't hurt to stretch the truth a bit.

Western novelist George Lyman perhaps was the first to recognize the wonderful possibilities of Julia's story. In the *Saga of the Comstock Lode* (1934), Lyman wrote, "All social life went on within her well-lighted, well-regulated, fragrant walls." He couldn't resist calling her small rented crib "Julia's Palace," which he described as the cultural center of the Comstock. The author maintained that Julia refined the city's ruffians by teaching them about fine French wines, cooking, and clothing, adding that she "caressed Sun Mountain with a gentle touch of splendor." Also, Lyman would not allow his heroine to simply walk the streets of Virginia City. He promoted the story that the wealthy courtesan "rode in a lacquered brougham upon whose side-panels were emblazoned her crest—an escutcheon of four aces, crowned by a lion couchant."

Lucius Beebe and Charles Clegg, Virginia City residents and owners of the *Territorial Enterprise,* wrote about Julia in *Legends of the Comstock Lode* (1950). They liked the story about the carriage, adding that it "had been imported across the Isthmus of Panama."

When Zeke Daniels (a.k.a. Effie Mona Mack of Reno) wrote the book *The Life and Death of Julia C. Bulette* (1958), she was skeptical about the "lacquered brougham." Daniels, however, elevated Bulette to the position of madam, calling her "the queen" of Virginia City's sporting row.

With the inventive assistance of those modern biographers, Julia assumed nursing capabilities second only to Florence Nightingale. Daniels asserted that Bulette never refused to help a sick miner. Beebe and Clegg wrote that Bulette nursed hundreds of disabled miners through bouts of influenza, using medicine culled from "the primitive resources of the community." They wrote that the miners gladly rallied to her support when hostile Paiute Indians threatened to attack the city. This bit of creative fiction became an important part of Julia's legend, despite the fact that the story was based on an incident that occurred several years before on the Comstock.

Julia's story received an additional boost in the 1950s when attention focused on her grave, or on a facsimile of it.

Bulette's original burial site had disappeared over the years, but some enterprising Virginia City residents found a way to make something out of nothing. They created a gravesite complete with white picket fence and placed it east of town among the ruins of the old Flowery Hill Cemetery. Tourists loved the idea. Since then Virginia City merchants also have named restaurants, saloons, and museums in her honor.

The stories, however, betray the reality of her existence. Recently, authors such as Marion Goldman and Douglas McDonald have worked to dispel the myths developed by earlier writers. In *The Legend of Julia Bulette* (1980), McDonald points out that contrary to previous descriptions of her "pleasure palace," Julia resided in one of the hastily-constructed cribs which lined Virginia City's D Street. Both biographers note that the preparation of sumptuous French meals would have been difficult in a house that lacked a kitchen and indoor plumbing, not to mention a French maid. Julia paid her neighbor Gertrude Holmes a small sum in return for meals. Her only helper was a Chinese man who came by on winter mornings to make a fire and sweep the floors. Goldman, in *Gold Digger and Silver Miners* (1981), states that the Comstock's most celebrated prostitute died in debt, leaving behind too many bills and not enough assets to cover them.

Undoubtedly, Julia would have been happy with a quarter of the wealth and honors that writers later attributed to her. Like other legends, her story gradually grew in details, each more exaggerated than the last, that added heroism and splendor to a hard life. The legend of Julia Bulette may be filled with inaccuracies, but it is a good story, whose embroideries make it one of the most captivating examples of Comstock folklore. It shows, at least at first, what residents were willing to believe about their disreputable neighbors when they had chance.

THE GREAT TRAIN ROBBERY

The West's first train robbery was a work of daring and criminal genius,
but the robbers left behind a few too many tracks.

(Originally appeared in May/June 1986)

By Terri Sprenger-Farley

ILLUSTRATION: DAN McNAMARA

It was about midnight on November 4, 1870, when the
Central Pacific's Atlantic Express slowed for Verdi. The
conductor stepped onto an open car platform for a breath
of air—and stopped. The bell cord was cut.

He squinted to be sure and then swung back toward the
engine. Facing him were three men in black masks.

Two more figures scrambled over the tender's woodpile and
dropped into the engine compartment. Six-shooters slid from
holsters, and a voice ordered the engineer to slow the train.

Silhouetted against a moonlit doorway, one masked man used his gun to motion the engineer, Henry S. Small, and his fireman down from their posts. He followed them to the door of the express car, knocked, and stepped back.

"Who's there?" asked the Wells Fargo guard inside.

"Engineer Small," came the reply.

When the guard opened the door, he was staring at three steady revolvers.

Seconds later the loot was divided.

"We're glad we didn't have to kill you," one of the bandits said to the guard.

Then all six were in the saddle.

"Ride like hell!" yelled the leader, jerking his mask free as he disappeared in the dark.

That night the six horsemen rode off with more than $40,000 in gold. They also earned themselves a large measure of fame, as newspapers soon told the nation how the gang had pulled off the first train robbery in the Western U.S.

Such daring should have meant the gang members would live to old age in wealth. And that might have happened if it hadn't been for a nervous robber and a red horse named Cockedoodle.

The robbery was Smiling Jack Davis' idea, spun out while he pretended respectability in Gold Hill. Manager of a livery stable and recorder for the Flowery Mining District on the outskirts of Virginia City, Davis also taught Sunday school and ran a small mill in Six Mile Canyon.

His success mystified those who didn't know that Davis mined the bulk of his profits from stagecoaches on Geiger Grade.

In planning the great railway heist, Davis couldn't figure why such a robbery hadn't been tried before—but he was confident. He rounded up three old road agent buddies, Tilton Cockerell, John Squires, and E.N. Parsons. A rider named Sol Jones was recommended by Chat Roberts, a friend who managed a stagecoach station. The least experienced member of the band was James Gilchrist. A miner like Davis, though a sight poorer, Gilchrist was a novice determined to make good in the highwayman's world.

On October 25, Davis' friend J.H. Chapman left Reno for San Francisco. Supplied with a special code that Davis had devised, Chapman nosed around. Then he heard about the November 4 train through Verdi: It would be carrying the payroll for Gold Hill's rich Yellow Jacket Mine.

Davis and his henchmen set up camp north of Reno near Peavine Mountain, where they stockpiled shotguns, six-shooters, and masks. To keep the boys happy, Davis brought them good food from Reno's Capitol House, where he ran the saloon. One day Davis was on such an errand when Sol Jones ran into the hideout, yelling, "I've got it, Jack!" He had the telegram:

"San Francisco November 1870

"S. Jones. Send me sixty dollars, if possible and oblige, (signed) Joseph Enrique."

Davis read it again. "Sixty" meant the treasure had only six guards. He smiled at the men around him. They'd be more than a match for those railroaders. The gray fall day turned bright as a birthday party.

On the appointed day Jones went to town for horses, and by the time he returned, the others were set to go. Tilton Cockerell took the red horse named Cockedoodle, and the gang set out for the old stone quarry at Lawton Hot Springs, six miles west of Reno. After days spent waiting, the men eagerly blocked the tracks with a stack of railroad ties and rocks. By nightfall it was ready.

Jones staked the horses so they could be released quickly and watched the others hike up the tracks to Verdi, four miles farther west. Being a boss had its advantages. Jones hunkered down on heels to wait. In less than an hour, he figured, he'd be rich.

Central Pacific No. 1 was pulling out of Verdi for the down-hill run into Reno when the rest of Davis' gang jumped aboard and directed Engineer Small to ease back on the throttle.

Seconds later the engine seemed to lean forward and glide a bit faster. The engineer saw the eyes above the black masks exchange looks of jubilation, and then he understood. The express car full of money, along with the engine and the ten-der, were free, uncoupled from the rest of the train.

Engineer Small saw the gang's barricade and brought the engine to a stop. He cooperated, but it galled him to escort the outlaws into the car, right past Frank Marshall, the guard from Wells Fargo.

"Give us the treasure and we will not hurt you," one robber promised.

Marshal watched as they axed open the money boxes and found $41,600 in $20 gold pieces, which they bagged and threw through the door. The robbers bemoaned having to leave behind more than $8,000 in silver bars because they were too heavy to carry, and thanked Marshall for refraining from a show of heroism that would have gotten him killed.

As they swung down from the train, they could see the rest of the cars coasting back to the engine. The train would be recoupled and reach Reno in minutes, and then the telegraph lines would sing.

The horsemen hit their saddles and rode whooping into the darkness.

Ever since stagecoaches began carrying Western payrolls and mine profits, the Wells Fargo guards, riding shotgun, had shown themselves as tough as the outlaws. "By God and by Wells Fargo," was the slogan used by the company bankers, but highway robbers knew another: "Wells Fargo Never Forgets."

As he had watched Jack Davis' band of robbers throw the heavy sacks of gold through the door, Frank Marshall had not been contemplating the gun poked in his ribs. He'd been watching his reputation fly into the night. And there was only one way to save it—find the culprits.

When the train arrived in Reno, Marshall wired San Francisco for help, and soon every lawman in Northern Nevada had joined the hunt.

"No further news in regard to the great robbery on the Central Pacific Railroad yesterday morning," Virginia City's *Territorial Enterprise* said. "The officers who went to the scene . . . have not yet returned or been heard from."

No doubt those local lawmen had heard what half the country knew. The prize for capturing the West's first train robbers was rich: Wells Fargo offered $10,000 for the robbers, Nevada Governor Henry G. Blasdel put up $20,000, and the U.S. Post Office threw in another $500.

The robbery site swarmed with trackers. Among them were Marshall and another Wells Fargo agent, C.C. Pendergast.

But it was Washoe County Undersheriff James H. Kinkead of Reno who single-handedly captured half the gang.

Although gang members Gilchrist, Parsons, and Squires had split up after the robbery, they spent the night in the same hotel in Sardine Valley, about 10 miles west of Verdi. Parsons and Squires left at daybreak, but Gilchrist, the novice, woke to hear Undersheriff Kinkead inquiring about suspicious guests.

When Kinkead rode off, the robber bolted from the outhouse, and the innkeeper's wife saw him sprint from there to his horse. She started calling out, but then stopped. On a hunch she hurried to the privy with a candle and found part of Gilchrist's hidden treasure—$120 in gold coins.

Kinkead soon caught up with Gilchrist and herded him into the Truckee jail, where he became the first to start unraveling the perfect crime. First Gilchrist said he lived in Meadow Lake, but he couldn't say where. And maybe he'd spent the night before last in a casino. Maybe. After prodding from Kinkead, however, he confessed to the robbery and told the lawman where to look for Squires and Parsons.

Following Gilchrist's clues, Kinkead inquired at a Loyalton hotel and was told an armed stranger was sleeping upstairs. It turned out to be Parsons. Spurred on by thoughts of reward money, Kinkead stopped the same day at Squires' brother's ranch—and found the third robber.

Further interrogation broke Gilchrist completely. He revealed the names of everyone involved in the plot.

Shortly afterward, Tilton Cockerell was arrested in a saloon north of Reno. Chat Roberts was taken at his stage station. A Wells Fargo detective found Sol Jones at the cabin of a gambler friend. Chapman, the San Francisco snoop, had just climbed down from the train and was headed to a nearby saloon for a celebratory drink when he, too, was nabbed.

Smiling Jack Davis showed himself all over Virginia City. He thought he'd make it plain he had nothing to hide. But he was under surveillance.

When his tail, Deputy Merrow, was sent to make his arrest, he was shocked by a strange occurrence. Davis' teeth, "which are generally brilliantly white, turned blue," Merrow told the *Territorial Enterprise.*

When Merrow hauled the robber before Police Chief Downey, it happened again during an exchange between the chief and Davis.

"We seem to have one of the train robbers in custody," said Downey.

"I'll bet you $2.50 you haven't," smiled Davis.

"I'll bet you $2.50 that I have one of them right here in town."

"Where?" asked Davis.

"There!" Downey said, pointing at Davis.

Once more, Smiling Jack Davis' famous grin turned blue.

Jailed, the robbers showed little loyalty. They spilled the whole story and tripped over each other in a rush to lead authorities to their hidden treasure.

Gilchrist led lawmen to a canyon off the Honey Lake Road

and pointed out a ledge hiding his share. Jones described the Peavine Mountain cache, which held his $7,345. Davis made much of his reluctance, but he finally gave in. He led deputies to three large sage bushes 100 yards above Hunter's Bridge on the Truckee. One kick at the edge, and gold glinted in the soil. Soon, according to the *Enterprise*, "The twenties were scraped up by the double handfuls. . . Davis did not assist in this work, but stood by looking on—doubtless almost sick at heart to see his booty scratched to the last coin."

When the search ended, $3,000 was still missing, and rumor had it that Davis might know its whereabouts.

By December 20, the day the robbers' trial began, Davis' wild bunch had been curried up. "In fact," mused the *Enterprise*, "they were the finest looking men in the court—no disrespect to the attorneys."

Three of the spiffy defendants, Gilchrist, Jones, and Chat Roberts, turned state's evidence. And a certain red horse kept nudging his way into the courtroom, adding insult to incrimination.

Chat's son, J.C. Roberts remembered hiding some money for Jones and noticing Cockerell's horse, Cockedoodle.

"I saw Cockerell at Roberts' ranch after the robbery. He came out on horseback on the morning of the fifth of November," swore rancher George Evans. "The horse he rode was called Cockedoodle."

The robbers had probably ceased listening when the final witness, Wells Fargo's F.T. Burke, claimed, "I arrested Jones at Mapes Ranch . . . he was on horseback, leading a horse known as"—did the agent pause for groans from the gang?—"Cockedoodle."

Jail sentences came down fast. Gilchrist and Roberts went free for their testimony. Jones received five years in the state prison. Davis got 10 years, Chapman 18. Parsons and Squires were both sentenced to 20 years. Cockerell, the man on the red horse, received 22 years.

Less than a year after sentencing, Cockerell, Chapman, Parsons, and Squires joined in a bloody prison break. The warden was battered and a man in town died. All the escapees were eventually captured, although Parsons remained free for five years.

Jack Davis declined to join in the break. In fact, he was such a cooperative prisoner that he was paroled after only three years.

And $3,000 was still missing, recalled those who watched Davis leave. Perhaps he had stashed it away in Six Mile Canyon or on the Truckee River.

Davis worked the Virginia City mines once more, but two years after he was released he was dead, shot in the back by a Wells Fargo guard riding shotgun on a stagecoach carrying a shipment of gold.

Local men later ventured into Six Mile Canyon, to look for Davis' fabled gold cache. However, according to the *Territorial Enterprise*, a huge bearded ghost, laughing fiendishly, rose from the earth. The treasure hunters, terrified, chose to follow the advice offered by Davis himself a decade before.

They jammed their hats down over their ears, swung their ponies around, and rode like hell.

GUNFIGHTERS OF PIOCHE

In the late 1800s in Pioche, if you didn't pack a gun
you might as well pack and run.

(Originally appeared in September/October 1986)

By A.D. Hopkins

"I'm Cemetery Sam, and I'm a gunfighter from Pioche." Those words mark the entry of the term "gunfighter" into the American language. They were written in 1874 in a humorous newspaper story about a frontier blowhard.

It was natural for Cemetery Sam to claim Pioche as the scene of his exploits, for Pioche in the 1870s suffered as sanguinary reputation as any town in the West. Despite the current tendency to discredit romantic exaggerations about frontier gunfight-

The notorious Morgan Courtney.

ers, in the case of Pioche the romantics are closer to the truth than the de-bunkers. The town attracted, and even created, real gunfighters as proficient as the fictional creations of Clint Eastwood. And Pioche was not satisfied with mere pistol duels between two antagonists; there were at least two pitched battles with 10 or more participants shooting away at each other.

Pioche today is a friendly, somewhat sleepy community that survives as Lincoln County's seat and one of the rural Nevada's best historical attractions. The town's steep streets, its century-old courthouse and jail, its wooden opera house and high-ceilinged barrooms—all evoke the feeling that you have fallen through a hole in time and landed in an era most people see only in history books.

But 115 years ago Pioche was a wide-open boom town. It is often claimed that 72 people were killed there before anyone died of natural causes. The claim is not true—pneumonia and typhoid did take early victims—but Pioche certainly earned its violent reputation. Historians count more than 40 killings in Lincoln County between 1870 and 1875, with only two men punished. In 1870, the year for which population figures are most reliable, Pioche had five homicides among its 1,171 residents. The following year there were 11 killings.

Many mining camps had violent years, but Pioche had special reasons for its wealth and gunplay. Its silver discoveries were concentrated in a small area, and close quarters led to disputes. Furthermore, there was the lull between the ore's discovery in 1864 and its development in 1876. Mormon settlers staked the first claims, but church leaders ordered members to concentrate on farming. Soldiers passing through also staked claims but failed to work them. So the mines' developers sometimes had to defend title against earlier claimants.

If Pioche had enjoyed a strong system of justice, these disputes might have been resolved peacefully. But Lincoln County's government was weak and notoriously corrupt. In one court case both sides bribed the same jury by stuffing money in a boot lowered from the jury-room window. Under such circumstances an honest verdict wasn't always available even when paid for, so a mine owner's only meaningful insurance lay in the best guns he could hire.

The most famous killings of the early years resulted from the mining companies' employment of professional "fighters" or "roughs," as they were called. While it is true that the roughs did some killings while defending claims, more lead flew during the gunmen's off-duty hours. Both the *Pioche*

Record and a Lincoln County grand jury censured mining companies for hiring roughs and blamed that practice for the violence.

Charles Gracey, a mining engineer who helped develop Pioche, gave a reminiscence to the Nevada Historical Society in 1908. In it he explained how one killing led to another.

The Raymond and Ely Mining Company, for which Gracey worked, had a wise policy of peaceably obtaining all claims, even worthless ones, adjacent to its own to prevent claim jumping or litigation by neighbors. One such buffer claim was the Washington and Creole. Two brothers named Newland had a claim up the steep hillside from the Washington and Creole. They asked permission to dig a horizontal tunnel to their claim through the W & C, thereby avoiding the greater labor of sinking a vertical shaft. Raymond and Ely officers consented, partly because they believed the W & C worthless.

But the Newland brothers hit ore while tunneling through the W & C. According to Gracey, the ore produced $300 worth of silver per ton—a rich find at 1986 prices, and in 1870 it was on a par with King Solomon's mines.

The lawful owners, the Raymond and Ely Company, allowed the Newlands to lease and work with W & C for 30 days, and at the end of that time the company allowed the Newlands to continue using the tunnel to reach their claim. But as Gracey said, "A mountain of ore worth $300 a ton will worry anyone when it is in plain sight and everyone is allowed to see it."

One morning the citizens of Pioche looked up the hillside to see a fort made of mine timbers, erected in a single night around the mouth of the Washington and Creole tunnel. Inside the fort stood gunmen hired by the Newland brothers. The Newlands threatened the officers of the Raymond and Ely Company with death if they so much as set foot on the claim. Then the Newland brothers resumed taking out the high-grade ore, this time without paying for it. "There was no law in the country and no one to stop them," Gracey said.

About that time, he recalled, there showed up in town four "polite, gentlemanly fellows, all under 30 years of age." They were Morgan Courtney, Michael Casey, Barney Flood, and William Bethers. The four made a secret agreement with the Raymond and Ely Company to recapture the Washington and Creole in exchange for a written promise that the four could work for 30 days.

Soon a quantity of whiskey arrived at the fort. One version of the story says that the whiskey was delivered as if by mistake. The claim jumpers winked at each other and said, "This is the place, all right." They preceded to drink it with one hand and pat themselves on the back with the other.

Most of the guards were dead drunk at 3 a.m. on November 9, 1870, when the four conspirators stormed over the wall with pistols blazing. Gracey said, "They drove the others out and away from their arms. I heard the shots and saw one man fall, Snell by name, and I saw Casey take a rifle and knock a man down with it."

Snell was the only man killed in what was known as the Whiskey Fight, and Thompson and West's history of Nevada adds that 10 were wounded and two were thrown down a 70-foot shaft. The only attacker among the wounded was Courtney, and he wasn't seriously hurt.

The Washington and Creole was thus returned to its rightful owners, and the use of hired fighters, and even fortifications, had begun. The following May, W.R. Warnock was shot dead as he passed one of the forts. His killer was never convicted. By September 1872 the Raymond and Ely Mine had a number of fighters on the payroll, and when its miners and some from the adjacent Phenix Mine tunneled into ground claims by both, an underground gunfight with revolvers and rifles ensued. Because both forces were protected by barricades, only one man was killed, but the shooting continued off and on for 17 hours.

Who were these men who made Pioche's name a byword for

violence? They were drawn from the disadvantage classes of their times. Most were immigrants, and many had been driven from Europe by hunger during the Potato Famine of 1845-46. Some, like Morgan Courtney, came without the parents who might have helped them make a better life. Many of the fighters were Irishmen. Since these were times when signs advertising better jobs warned, "No Irish need apply," it is not surprising that Irish names are disproportionately numerous on the role of roughs.

Following just four gunfighters—Whiskey Fight heroes Courtney, Flood, Bethers, and Casey—we get a particularly good picture of what Pioche gunfighters were like and how they were made.

On February 22, 1871, three months after the Whiskey Fight, a miner named Thomas Coleman was stabbed to death. Barney Flood and Morgan Courtney were arrested but released for lack of evidence. Flood soon got in trouble for knifing another man—who did not die—and skipped town soon afterward and was killed in a gunfight in Eureka.

In the meantime, the rightful owners of the Washington and Creole had kept their promise to let the four work the rich claim for 30 days. Gracey says they made $60,000, which they divided among themselves, making them rich.

On the day they took the money to the bank, Mike Casey got into an argument with a man named Tom Gossen, and both drew guns. Gossen missed but Casey didn't. But before Gossen died, he gave away all his money except $5,000, which he left in trust for whoever killed Casey.

There was much argument in town about who was to blame for the Casey-Gossen gunfight. A miner named Jim Levy saw the fight and said Casey fired first. On May 30 Casey ran into Levy in a store and asked him if he had indeed saw that. Levy admitted he had, and Casey commenced abusing him.

"Levy said in a quiet way, 'You can abuse me now while you have your gun with you.' Casey told him to get his gun and come shooting," related Gracey.

Levy went home, armed himself, and returned. Casey and a friend, Dave Neagle, lay in wait for him, but Levy popped out of an alley and surprised both. Levy creased Neagle's skull with a bullet, wounded Casey with at least one more, and then closed in on Casey and beat him over the head with a pistol. Neagle continued to fire but hit Levy only once, in the chin, leaving a scar Levy would wear for life.

Casey died not of the bullet wound but of the pistol whipping. For Levy and Neagle, the event began their careers as two of the West's most noted gunfighters. Most of Neagle's was at least nominally on the side of the law. As a deputy under Sheriff Johnny Behan in Tombstone, Neagle was one of the few people who tried to cut the burning fuse before the Earp-Clanton feud blew up into total war. He killed more than one outlaw in other episodes, and for a time he was Tombstone's chief of police. The best known event of his life occurred in 1889, when he was United States Marshal, assigned to escort U.S. Supreme Court Justice Steven Field. David Terry, a prominent attorney and successful duelist, slapped Field in a train station, apparently trying to provoke a duel. Then Terry reached for a bowie knife, Neagle said, so he shot him dead. Ten years later Neagle came to Carson City in the service of U.S. Senator William Stewart, who was facing a stiff reelection challenge from Congressman Francis Newlands. The election was in the hands of the Nevada Legislature, and the former gunfighter helped persuade lawmakers to reelect the incumbent. Neagle was still alive in the 1920s, and presumably he died in bed.

Levy collected the $5,000 reward for killing Casey, and from that day forth he was a changed man—a gambler and a gunman. "Casey's friends were now the enemies of Levy and tried their best to kill him," Gracey said. "But he proved to be the most fearless and aggressive in that line that had ever appeared and was soon the terror of all the fighters." In a series of articles he wrote about gunfighting, Bat Masterson confirmed that assessment of Levy's nerve and skill. Levy was accused of firing the fatal shot in Pioche's underground fight but was never convicted. He died in Tucson in 1882, ambushed by men who were afraid to face him in a fair fight.

Courtney, considered the leader of the crew recaptured the Washington and Creole, continued to court trouble. He remained in Pioche and in June 1872 got into a barroom argument with a man named Sullivan. Sullivan followed him outside, drew a knife, and, according to Courtney, called him an S.O.B.—an accurate but unwise description. Courtney, safely out of range of Sullivan's knife, drew his revolver and ordered Sullivan to eat his words or die. Sullivan didn't take them back, and Courtney shot him through the heart.

Despite vigorous prosecution, a jury acquitted Courtney, probably because of the language Sullivan had used against him. The term "S.O.B." may be casually applied to friends today, but newspapers of the 1870s are full of evidence that it was then a fighting word.

As soon as the verdict was announced, Courtney was arrested again, this time for an 1868 murder in Virginia City. But luck was still with Courtney. The witnesses against him were miners who ran off to a new strike before the trial. They could not be found; the charges were dismissed.

So Courtney returned to Pioche in the spring of 1873—but why? The town must have been full of men who wanted to kill him for revenge or simply because he was "the chief"— Nevada's term at the time for top gun—and killing him would earn that crown.

Perhaps he returned because Pioche was the only place where Morgan Courtney had ever amounted to much. His heroic image had been sullied by his bloody deeds, and yet people still seemed to like him. He was a free spender. He belonged to two fire companies, which were important social organizations. Some say he helped raise money to build

Pioche's first Protestant Church, although he was Catholic.

So he came back and landed a job as superintendent of a mine. He also landed a girlfriend named Georgie Scyphers. She was a prostitute with a tough streak. When one customer assaulted her, she shot him in the arm. Several years later she killed a man for defaming her sister.

The other man in Georgie's life, not counting paying customers, was James McKinney. He was a gambler and was reputedly addicted to both whiskey and laudanum, the heroin of the 19th century.

As one would expect, Courtney and McKinney crossed paths. Georgie Scyphers later testified that McKinney grew angry because she broke a date with him on the night of August 1, 1873. McKinney denied that story. He said that Courtney was jealous and called him various names, names that even today read rough in court documents.

McKinney and other witnesses claimed Courtney had ordered McKinney to leave town or die. But McKinney couldn't leave town; he was suffering from serious intestinal blockage and was unfit to travel by horseback or stage.

It may have been that McKinney decided it was better to die from Courtney's bullet than from a forced journey. It may have been simply that a man with blocked intestines is apt to be cranky. But McKinney borrowed a pistol and went looking for Courtney. When he found him, he fired six shots, hitting Courtney with five. Courtney tried to draw his own gun, but his arm had been disabled, and by the time he could draw it a policeman was dragging McKinney to jail.

The shots had been fired at such close range that Courtney's linen was burning, and passersby tore it from him and trod the fire into the dirt street. Then they carried him into a nearby drugstore, where a doctor examined him and told him he would not live. Courtney dictated a dying statement, which was recorded in pencil on a piece of writing paper.

The statement said who shot him and who gave McKinney the pistol and how Courtney knew who gave it to him. It even explained why Courtney did not defend himself.

What it did not express was a single regret for the deaths of Snell, Sullivan, the man in Virginia City, or any of the others Courtney was suspected of killing. It contained not one word of love for Georgie Scyphers, the woman over whom he had fought. Between the coldness of his dying words and the ease with which he could switch from boon to companion to bully, we see the personality of a sociopath.

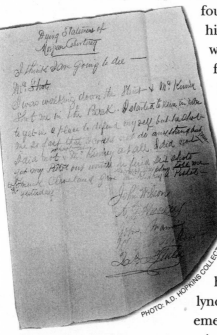

PHOTO: A.D. HOPKINS COLLECTION

Morgan Courtney's dying statement was discovered 100 years later.

Morgan Courtney got a hero's funeral. A brass band and the fire companies marched in the procession, followed by most of the people in town.

During McKinney's trial there was talk of lynching him, but nobody was ever lynched in Pioche despite the emergence of a vigilance committee about this time. McKinney was finally acquitted, partly due to Courtney's choice of threatening language—ironically, the same defense that Courtney had used in the Sullivan case.

McKinney stayed out of trouble after shooting Courtney. He apparently got well, overcame his addiction to laudanum, and was said to still be alive in 1908.

Courtney's killing wasn't the last in the chain that started at the W & C. John Manning, a friend of the late gunman, picked a fight with a big policeman named W.L. "Fat Mac" McKee, implying that Mac had set Courtney up. McKee tried to brush him off, but Manning went for a gun. According to the *Pioche Record*, McKee outdrew him, with consequences fatal to Manning.

Dime novels aside, this is the only reliable report the author has ever seen of one gunman outdrawing another who started to draw first. Possibly Manning was drunk and McKee sober. Also, Manning had to reach under his coat for his revolver, and it probably was a single-action, which could be fired only by pulling the hammer back before pulling the trigger. McKee carried a double-action revolver, which, like most modern revolvers, could be fired quickly without cocking the hammer. However McKee accomplished his feat, he was admired for it; he later was elected sheriff.

The firearms used by Pioche gunmen are another point in which folklore has departed considerably from reality. It has been written that Courtney arrived in Pioche in 1870 wearing a pair of low-slung Colt .45s, which is demonstrably untrue because the Colt .45 wasn't made until 1873. He did carry a Colt, but it was probably a percussion Navy or pocket model. It had to be reasonably compact because he carried it in his right coat pocket.

Nor were percussion Colts as popular with early gunmen as generally believed. Stories of gunfights in Nevada newspapers of the late 1860s and early '70s frequently mentioned revolvers, particularly Whistlers, which apparently were double-action types.

Because the gunfighting era in Pioche lasted only through 1873, its weapons were percussion arms, firing round balls that needed to be placed with more precision than did the more powerful .45 slugs that came later. So the Pioche gunfighters aimed carefully. Except for the confrontation between McKee and Manning, the outcome of gunfighters did not depend on who could draw a gun fastest. If an invitation to "go into the street" was accepted, the gun might be drawn even before going outside and pointed downward until the antagonists had reached a reasonable distance to open fire.

But that such invitations were commonly given and commonly accepted there can be no doubt. The men who gave them were different from us in an important respect—they grew up in a world in which personal violence was accepted. Only a few years earlier the formal duel had been common in both the United States and Ireland. Personal courage was still valued highly.

Perhaps these men valued courage more than most, for so much of it had been required of them. They were, after all, children of the Potato Famine, come of age during the Civil War. And they made their marks in Pioche, the mining camp where you could become rich, famous, and highly sought after—by both clients and rivals—as a gunfighter.

GHOST TOWN RAMBLER

In Nevada's old mining camps, the dreams linger on.

(Originally appeared in May/June 1988)

By Richard Moreno

PHOTO: RICHARD T. STEPHENS

Rhyolite, near Death Valley, is one of the state's most picturesque ghost towns.

It was a brisk spring day in Belmont, and my friend Wes and I were walking near the ruins of the stamp mill at the west end of the old mining town.

"Listen," Wes said suddenly. "Can you hear it?"

I tilted my head and heard a faint flapping noise, somewhat like the sound made when you cup your hand and slap it on water. The sound grew louder, then moved away.

"What was that?"

Wes pointed to the sky. Above, I saw two birds landing on a branch in a nearby cottonwood tree.

"It's so quiet and peaceful here," he said with a touch of awe, "that you can hear a bird's wings flapping."

I am reminded of that moment every time I visit a Nevada ghost town. When I heard those birds in Belmont, and Wes' quiet explanation, it made me realize just how strange it feels to be alone in a forgotten town.

Most people in our society rarely have the chance—or make the time—to truly get away from it all. During the day, we spend our time in atmosphere-controlled offices filled with the hum of machines and air-treatment systems. Outside, we are inundated by the noise of automobiles and other people.

There is an easy peace in a town that once thrived but is now at rest. In the old days the town's dirt streets were crowded with horses and wagons. The saloons were noisy with scruffy prospectors and dirt-caked cowboys. Now you can hear birds in flight.

For the most part, Nevada's 19th-century mining towns were disposable communities created long before disposable razors and lighters. They were founded on promises and dreams, and when those hopes went unfulfilled—or the rich ore finally gave out—the towns were left to bask in the sun and wind.

It is estimated there is at least one ghost town for every living town in Nevada. For every Las Vegas, Reno, or Gabbs, there is a Metropolis, Rawhide, or Cherry Creek.

The reason for the remarkable rise and fall of those towns can be traced to the ephemeral nature of the mining industry. A mining boom lasts as long as ore is available. Then, usually, comes the bust.

Throughout the Silver State the same cycle played out in scores of cities and hamlets: Rich ore was discovered, miners flocked to the area hoping to get rich, a town and its services developed, the ore ran out, and the town ceased to have a reason to exist.

Not every mining town disappeared when the ore was gone. Some, like Virginia City, Tonopah, and Ely, were forced to retrench but survived because they were located on a major road, found new industries, or were able to attract tourists who appreciated the towns' colorful pasts.

Others, like Goldfield and Gold Point, were on their way to oblivion but have been rescued in recent times by residents and newcomers who refused to allow the towns to die.

A case in point is Goldfield, which was Nevada's largest city in 1909 when it boasted more than 20,000 residents. But just as nature brought good fortune to Goldfield, so did it harass the young desert city. There were floods, like the one in 1913 that destroyed one-third of the town. Fires were equally destructive, like the 1923 conflagration that destroyed 54 city blocks. Finally, neglect threatened to reduce the historic town to a faded memory.

But some residents remained, holding fast to important reminders of the town's heritage such as the old homes, the Esmeralda County Courthouse, and the Goldfield Hotel, which was built in 1907-08. While the town is perhaps a bit frayed around the edges, Goldfield's residents enthusiastically usher visitors around the aging ruins and have ensured it will never become a true ghost.

Another resurrection has taken place at a lesser known mining town, Gold Point, 30 miles south of Goldfield. First called Lime Point and then Hornsilver, the town got a new name when gold was found there in 1927.

Gold Point's recent revival, as a tourist attraction, is headed by Herb Robbins, a wallpaper hanger from Las Vegas, who used to spend his vacations visiting ghost towns all over Nevada. When he discovered Gold Point in 1978, Robbins liked its mystical feeling of old wood and space—and decided to buy some of the buildings. For the past 15 years, he and other residents have been slowly restoring Gold Point. For example, the Hornsilver Town Site and Telephone Company building, which was the old real estate office, has been converted to a saloon. In recent years, a wild animal preserve has been started by other residents of the town.

But for every Goldfield and Gold Point, there are dozens of

towns that have disappeared.

As befits disposable towns, some were in part dismantled, with the pieces moved to other locations. The International Hotel in Austin, for example, was brought from Virginia City while the picturesque wooden church in Manhattan was originally located in Belmont.

Other towns gradually disappeared as weather, vandals, and scavengers probably had the most damning effect on many once-robust towns. Nevada's ghost town lore is filled with tales of people, often well intentioned, removing furniture, stoves, wood, bricks, foundations—even tombstones—for building materials or souvenirs.

A hardy handful of towns have survived, however, because they were never completely abandoned. Fortunately, the last remaining residents (or in some cases, resident) would serve as guardian angels, watching over the town and fending off intruders who sought to take home a piece of its past.

For instance, in Belmont visitors are often greeted by one of the town's guardian angels. He or she will be courteous and friendly, but firm about one thing—you can look all you want, but don't touch anything.

On a recent photography trip I was met on Belmont's main street by a man who asked my business and then graciously pointed out a few buildings I might like to photograph.

Photogenic but isolated, Belmont was founded in 1865, when silver was discovered nearby. In two years, the town had 2,000 residents and was the Nye County seat. But the ore began to thin out, and in 1905, Belmont lost the county seat to Tonopah. Soon Belmont had streets lined with abandoned buildings and a population you could count on one hand.

Today it takes two hands to count the town's residents, and there is a saloon that is open during the summer months, but otherwise Belmont is hardly threatened by progress. Walking the streets, you can recognize what was once a substantial community. The main drag is lined with the brick, stone, and wooden facades of old buildings including the former bank and general store. Across the way, the two-story Cosmopolitan Saloon has fallen down—the result of vandalism.

The hills are littered with the walls and foundations of homes and other buildings, including the impressive Belmont Courthouse, built in 1876 and partially restored by the Nevada Division of State Parks. To the south and west of the main part of the town are the massive brick ruins of the stamp mills that once processed ore from the local mines.

Each of Nevada's ghost towns has a unique mood. While Belmont is peaceful, Rhyolite has a more stark and haunting quality. Located near Beatty on the edge of Death Valley National Park, Rhyolite has suffered the indignities of harsh desert, neglect, and scavengers.

Yet, I find that the hard times have given Rhyolite character, like the deep, sunburnt lines on the face of an old prospector.

Established in 1905, the town quickly grew to more than 6,000 people. It had three railroad lines, a stock exchange, and blocks of substantial stone buildings.

But the Nevada mining cycle repeated itself. The ore ran out, people moved away, and by the 1930s Rhyolite was a ghost town. Many of the structures became building material for newer towns. Other buildings were worn by the hard Amargosa winds. A few, like a house made of bottles and the mission-style railroad depot, have survived because steps have been taken to preserve them.

The best time to visit Rhyolite is late afternoon when the sun is low and the shadows are long. The twilight softens the hills' jagged edges and bathes the town in rich tones that provide beautiful photographic opportunities.

Equally vacant and haunting are the ruins of Delamar, a Southeastern Nevada mining town whose deadly dust gave it a nickname: the Widowmaker.

Reached by a rough and occasionally perilous dirt road, Delamar is about 25 miles southwest of Caliente and 15 miles south of U.S. 93. The town gained notoriety because its mines used a dry drilling process that produced a fine dust, giving many workers silicosis.

Despite that danger, Delamar grew to 3,000 citizens at the turn of the century. The mines produced for another 10 years before tapping out, or reaching "borrasca," as miners call it. By the mid-1930s, Delamar was empty. Many of Delamar's wooden buildings had been transported on wagons from Pioche; they were moved back when Delamar declined.

The road to Delamar, which is strewn with boulders and in places runs along the edge of a cliff, requires a four-wheel-drive vehicle. I've found no complete buildings, but there are plenty of walls and foundations to explore. Overlooking the ruins are massive mounds of tailings, large holes, and abandoned mine shafts—grim reminders of the Widowmaker's heyday.

Most of Nevada's ghost towns are not as forbidding. Unionville, for instance, is set in a secluded, picturesque canyon.

The first time I traveled to Unionville I learned that first appearances can be deceiving. Between Lovelock and Winnemucca on Interstate 80, I turned south at the Mill City exit and drove 17 miles through a dry, brown valley.

A historical marker indicated that Unionville was three miles west on a good dirt road. I followed the road past a few irrigated fields, thinking I was headed for the end of the world. Instead, Unionville turned out to be an oasis. A small creek ran through Buena Vista Canyon, providing a bucolic setting with tall trees, shrubs, and green grass.

There were about a dozen homes sprouting from the ruins of the old town, including the Pioneer Garden, a quaint bed-and-breakfast inn. At the end of the road, I parked near the creek and hiked for several miles through lush vegetation on the old road that parallels the creek. As the sun reached its zenith, I returned to explore (politely) the town.

PHOTO: RICHARD MORENO

This fixer-upper symbolizes Nevada's boom-and-bust past.

Unionville was established in 1861 and was briefly called Dixie until Union sympathizers took control. For a short time the town was the Humboldt County seat, a distinction passed on to Winnemucca in 1873.

Unionville was the home of young Samuel Clemens for three weeks in 1862. After trying his hand at mining, Clemens moved on to Virginia City, where he began writing under the name Mark Twain.

While mining is a thing of the past in Unionville, in Tuscarora—set in the cattle country of Elko County—mining keeps coming back. For several years, large microscopic-gold mines have operated to the north, giving Nevada new life as a gold producer. Closer to home, Tuscarora's handful of full-time residents live with an open-pit mine nipping at their town's south end.

Gold was discovered there in the 1860s, and at one time 4,000 people were mining and prospecting the area. After the ore ran out, Tuscarora, like Belmont and Unionville, was never completely abandoned. In recent years Tuscarora has become noted for artist Dennis Parks' pottery school. Set among the town's old wooden buildings are a number of modern trailers and shiny mobile homes, a sign of the town's annual summer population boom, to 30. Despite the influx of the summer fishing crowd, the Tuscarora Tavern has closed, so the nearest saloon is now at Taylor Canyon, seven miles east at the paved road.

A different kind of ghost town can be found at Berlin, 23 miles east of Gabbs and part of Berlin Ichthyosaur State Park. Like many Nevada mining camps, Berlin grew on the side of a mountain. Unlike any others, Berlin is owned and protected by the state.

Founded at the turn of the century, Berlin faded after 1909, but the buildings were protected by the mining company. In the 1970s, the Nevada Division of State Parks acquired the town and has maintained its mill, several homes, and a few commercial buildings in what preservationists call "a state of arrested decay." The park also contains paleontological reminders of the state's past—namely the fossils of ichthyosaurs, huge fish-like creatures from the Age of Dinosaurs.

While Berlin's ride to glory was brief, Cherry Creek, 55 miles north of Ely, is a good example of a Nevada town that never could climb off the mining roller coaster.

The town's first silver boom occurred in 1872. The town then declined until new silver veins were uncovered in 1880. That boom lasted three years and was followed by another decline. The district revived in 1905 for a three-year ride and again in 1935 for a five-year spurt.

Despite the ups and downs, Cherry Creek has survived. In fact, a few modern-day miners continue to work the area and believe it's ripe for a fifth ride. The most picturesque building in the little town is the old Western-style saloon, which is open when the owner is inclined.

The surrounding landscape is littered with the remains of the various mining booms, including some camera-worthy head frames, old miners' shacks, and the mounds of tailings. Other ghosts tell the area's story best: The various mining booms are reflected in the dates carved on tombstones in the Cherry Creek cemetery.

Time and neglect have ravaged ghost towns throughout Nevada. Yet life in those once-bustling cities somehow remains timeless.

I fondly remember that when I climbed into my car to leave Belmont, the town's self-appointed guardian angel appeared from his trailer to ask if I could please tell him the time.

After I answered, he paused. Then he asked if I knew what day it was.

That's timeless all right.

THE FIRST BLACK RANCHER

Ben Palmer and a group of black pioneers made their marks in the 1800s.

(Originally appeared in January/February 1989)

By Ed Johnson and Elmer R. Rusco

In 1891 the *Genoa Weekly Courier* reported an incident that involved a prominent Carson Valley rancher: "As Ben Palmer was driving . . . Tuesday with a span of light-footed Bonners, the nut dropped off the front wheel in Jacks Valley and the wheel running off, the driver was thrown to the ground with a man on top of him. The team went like a flash, but Ben with his born grit, clung to the ribbons and soon hauled them up and was himself but slightly bruised. Ben is a stayer."

Clearly, Ben Palmer was a skilled and determined man who knew horses. Also, as the newspaper's readers would know, Palmer was black. In fact, he was one of a small group of black ranchers who were important residents of the valley in the 19th century and, most likely, the first black settlers in Nevada.

Palmer, who claimed 320 acres of fine grassland south of Genoa in 1853, was among the area's earliest non-Indian settlers. The black drover came to what was then western Utah Territory with his sister Charlotte and her family. Charlotte was married to a white man, David (or D.H.) Barber, and the family settled next door to Palmer on 400 acres of land in the same year. Benjamin, one of the Barbers' seven children, was the first non-Indian born in the Carson Valley. According to the 1900 census, Benjamin Barber was born in Nevada in 1853. The first white child born in the valley, Louisa Beatrice Mott, was born December 10, 1854.

Ben Palmer became one of the most successful ranchers in the valley and "left one of the finest farms . . . as a monument," the *Gardnerville Record-Courier* observed in 1908. Palmer, whose

Carson Valley rancher Ben Palmer with resident Mary Hawkins in the late 1800s.

last name was sometimes misspelled Parmer, was described by Virginia City's *Territorial Enterprise* in 1867 as "one of the heaviest taxpayers in Douglas County," and the tax records show that was true. In 1857 he was not only on the list of the 47 largest taxpayers—those with assessed valuations of $5,000 or more—but also ranked 10th in the value of his property. His holdings in the Sheridan area were worth more than those of many prominent white residents such as John S. Childs, Fred Dressler, and Henry and P.W. Van Sickle.

A busy cattleman, Palmer drove 1,500 head from Seattle to Carson Valley in 1857 to replenish his herd, and the next year a newspaper reported, "Ben Parmer's cattle—450 head—passed through Genoa last Tuesday on their way to Goose Lake, Oregon." It was said that he introduced Bonner horses, a breed that is seldom heard of today, to the area.

Charlotte's husband David died in 1873, and their son, Benjamin Barber, ran the Barbers' ranch for 30 years. While

their ranch was not as profitable as Palmer's, it was a successful operation, assessed at levels ranging from $2,000 to $5,245
between 1883 and 1914.

By 1860 a third black family consisting of Winfield and
Sophia Miller and their children had a ranch adjacent to
Palmer and the Barbers. Although Winfield died in the 1860s,
Sophia maintained the ranch for many years. Longtime local
rancher Fred Dressler said in his 1984 oral history that "everybody admired Winfield because he could really ride a horse.
They used to say he could put two 50-cent pieces on the bot-
tom of his stirrup and never lose those 50-cent pieces under
his toes and ride the bucking horse to the finish."

The black ranchers employed black, Indian, and white
ranch hands, and there were other black people living Carson
Valley in the 1800s.

Early Nevada law discriminated against all non-whites. For
example, only whites could vote until 1870. But there is evidence that these black ranchers were highly respected. After
1870 Ben Palmer and Benjamin Barber were regularly regis-
tered to vote. In at least 1876 and 1878 Palmer was a member
of the Douglas County Grand Jury, and in the latter year he
was named to the panel of trial jurors.

Palmer and the Barbers were known and remembered for
their hospitality. An article reporting Charlotte's death in
1887 noted that her funeral procession "was one of the largest
ever witnessed in Douglas county" and went on to say of "this
excellent woman" that "she was very charitable," and "at her
house no one was ever denied a meal or a night's lodging."

The black ranchers also were respected simply because they
were good citizens. In 1877 Palmer played a role in appre-
hending a murder suspect. When a man named Peter Wilson
was stabbed to death in Dutch Valley, just across the state line
in California, the chief suspect rode away on his horse but
turned his mount loose at the Miller ranch and tried to hide
in a hay mow. The horse was found at Palmer's ranch, and

Palmer and another man were able to follow the horse's tracks back to the hay mow. There, Palmer talked the suspect into surrendering to the justice of the peace.

One of the Barbers' sons, Lyman, became a successful rancher just south of Carson Valley in California. Like his Uncle Ben, Lyman had a knack for posse work. In 1879 he helped a fellow named C.H. Kilgore chase and capture a young man who had robbed Kilgore at gunpoint on the road from Bodie.

Palmer died in 1908 at the age of 82. After his nephew Benjamin died in 1925, only one of Charlotte's children, Clarissa Church, was still alive. In 1928 Clarissa was visited by Abe Nathan, a leading merchant in the valley for many years who had moved to the state of Washington. During his visit, the *Gardnerville Record-Courier* reported, Nathan "spent a day renewing acquaintanceships, including Miss Clarissa Church and others. One of Mr. Nathan's fond remembrances is when he rode horseback with the late Ben Parmer and he visited the old ranch near Sheridan where his happy boyhood days were spent."

Today, two monuments remind us of these early black pioneers. In the northeast corner of the Mottsville cemetery, which sits six miles south of Genoa in the shadow of Job's Peak, there is a neat plot with a central monument and a number of tombstones surrounded by a low concrete wall. Here lie Ben Palmer, Charlotte and David Barber, and their seven children.

Two miles south of the cemetery Ben Palmer's sturdy barn still stands, bearing witness to the presence of black settlers in this beautiful valley, the first stopping place of the people who built modern Nevada.

DAT SO LA LEE AND THE MYTH WEAVERS

The Washoe basket maker's fine weavings ensured her legendary status, but her patrons, Abe and Amy Cohn, reinforced it with lies that still live on.

(Originally appeared in September/October 1989)

By Christopher Ross

CARSON CITY NEWS, OCTOBER 7, 1911:

"Abe Cohn is in serious trouble once again! Mrs. Louisa Keyser [Dat So La Lee], the well known artist, gives tongue lashing to manager of the Emporium. Last evening, when the Glenbrook stage arrived, a big fat squaw was unloaded with the assistance of several men, and after she had been safely landed on terra firma, she gave a grunt of satisfaction and bundled herself off to give a lecture to Abe Cohn on the ways of the White people and the way she was abused. Cohn saved himself from the tirade by handing the buxom lady a half dollar and vanishing out the back door of his store ...

"For the next few days it will be comical to watch the antics of Cohn, for Mrs. Keyser came down from Glenbrook last night, mad as a march hare, and life will not be sweet for Abe until he has managed to explain to her that only one seat in a stage can be given to any one passenger."

Dat So La Lee

This jocular but racist report was typical of published accounts about the great Washoe Indian basket weaver Dat So La Lee. Most of these stories dealt with her supposed ignorance and misunderstandings with Abe Cohn, her

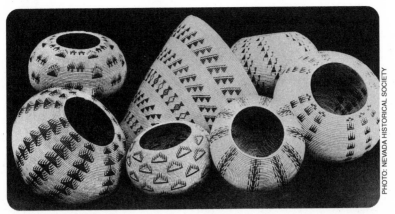

Amy Cohn created elaborate myths to describe Dat So La Lee's elegant designs.

patron. Today, the accepted history of her life is based on such articles and on information published by the Emporium, Cohn's business in Carson City, and each year such accounts are republished and discussed.

These so-called facts, which enjoy wide circulation, have one thing in common—they are complete fabrications. Although they give us clues about relations between whites and Indians in turn-of the-century Nevada and between Abe and his wife Amy, the stories and data that have been so studied and preserved are, almost without exception, blatant lies.

The myths were the result of an unusual collaboration between the Cohns. While Abe seemed to appreciate Dat So La Lee's work, his wife Amy was truly fascinated by the weaving at which Dat So La Lee excelled. Amy carefully recorded designs and wrote down meanings, and she documented Dat So La Lee's early history and the tribal culture before contact with whites. Her precise records of Washoe ceremonies stand in sharp contrast to the crude, derogatory anecdotes associated with her husband that have been extensively used by researchers.

Still, Amy's work is similar to her husband's in one way. It is also completely false, fabricated not merely to supplement or enliven the truth, but to hide and refute historical fact in favor of an invented romantic Anglo vision of Indian life.

Only recently has the true history of Washoe basket design, Dat So La Lee, and the Cohns of Carson City come to light, through the research of Dr. Marvin Cohodas, a Canadian and professor of anthropology at the University of British Columbia.

For years Cohodas has been the leading world authority on Washoe basketry, and his book *Degikup* is a standard reference. But more important, Cohodas knows basketry from an insider's point of view. He taught himself to weave after watching an Indian woman in Arizona: "Just a little watching and a lot of work," he says. Although he won't evaluate his own work, others place it as equal to that of the 10 greatest weavers not including Dat So La Lee, and his baskets are becoming collectible in their own right.

According to Cohodas, Dat So La Lee's story begins with her people, the Washoe, who were among the last Indians to encounter the whites in the mid-1800s. Inhabiting five of the richest valleys along the eastern Sierra, the Washoes enjoyed far-flung trade to the coast and the Mojave region. One of the traits that helped them survive was their ability to make a variety of baskets: burden baskets, water jugs, cradleboards, winnowing baskets, and others, in a variety of weaves, some related in technique and style to the California Miwok and others to Great Basin tribes.

The first whites in Western Nevada looked down on the Washoes. Although the Washoes often tried to drive whites off their lands, or at least be paid compensation, their warfare was nothing like that of the Plains and Rocky Mountain Indians. By the time of the Potato War of 1857, when a few Washoes were killed for stealing potatoes near Honey Lake, the Washoes were considered a nuisance.

In truth, the Washoes' culture had simply been destroyed by white settlers who preempted the fish, seed-bearing plants, and piñon pines on which the Indians depended. Cohodas points out that by the time the Washoe adjusted, they had basically become a servant class to ranchers, farmers, and city dwellers.

In time the Washoe abandoned most types of basketry because they found iron pots to be so superior for cooking. But ironware could not replace seed collectors, winnowers, and cradleboards, and a few Washoe women continued to weave utilitarian pieces into the 20th century. The collectors began buying Indian baskets.

"We don't know if a Washoe woman in, say, 1800, would make a lot of decoration on a basket she was planning to use in everyday life," Cohodas says in his usual cautious style. "All

Abe Cohn

PHOTO: NEVADA HISTORICAL SOCIETY

we know is that by 1895, at least some weavers were making baskets specially for sale, and using fancy designs. All baskets we have are after that date. There are no securely documented fancy baskets before 1895.

"People often brought baskets to Cohn's Emporium and said, 'This one is 80 years old—we've been using it for four generations.' But that seems unlikely. They probably only lasted one to two years in daily use, which is why almost everyone knew how to make them—they went through a lot of them."

Cohodas' statistical analyses of early styles also suggest that designs didn't develop much until the tourist trade.

So Washoe fancy basketry really developed only in the last 85 years of the 8,000 years of Great Basin basket making, and it did so despite an apparent gap between the prehistoric baskets and white-influenced ones. Cohodas says, "I'd like to know what a 19th-century basket looks like—I have never found or seen one."

By 1895, things were rough for the Washoes. There were many old, destitute, blind, and maimed among them. Their old pine-nut allotments were inadequate. Their original valley home sites were all taken by ranchers. Despite efforts by the whites to designate one, the Washoes had never had a real leader. Their biggest authority was the rabbit boss, who organized rabbit hunting drives.

Thus no one was particularly interested in their culture when Amy Cohn discovered that her washerwoman, Louisa Keyser, known in Washoe as Dat So La Lee, or "Big Hips," was a basket weaver. When she married Abe, Amy was a young widow with three daughters. She was a strong, well-educated woman with a vivid imagination, and she single-handedly resurrected Washoe weaving, in the process elevating it from a craft to an elaborate art with its own mythology.

Although the facts of the discovery of Dat So La Lee by the Cohns are hopelessly shrouded in myth, there is no doubt that in 1898 the Emporium began selling baskets shortly after moving to the center of what became known as the Emporium block, a site across the street from today's Carson Nugget.

By 1899, Amy was making up certificates for the baskets, using her interpretations of Dat So La Lee's designs. In 1900, she began to energetically promote Dat So La Lee and her work and soon had a permanent summer outlet at Tahoe City to take advantage of the tourist trade on Lake Tahoe's north shore.

By 1909, Amy was giving lectures while presenting the baskets as symbols of primordial life among the noble savages before the whites contaminated them. With Dat So La Lee sitting in the background, Amy gave her first such lecture to the local Leisure Hour Club. The local newspaper described the event, which included a reading of "Hiawatha":

"The picture in which Dat So La Lee posed was made trebly interesting because of two other figures. Mrs. Gladys Hofer, in a scarlet gown, recited an original poem by Mr. Vanderlieth in which the reasons for the designs in the basket were asked of the weaver. Her questions were answered by Mrs. Marguerite

Raycraft, who represented the daintiest Indian maiden imaginable, and who is always the personification of grace. The answer is also the product of Mr. Vanderlieth's fertile brain."

Cohodas comments, "In order to fully appreciate this juxtaposition of fantasy and reality, one must remember that Louisa Keyser was heavy-set and dressed in a print dress and scarf, and she did not generally speak well in public. The slender and graceful Marguerite Raycraft as the Indian princess explaining her symbolism represented the antithesis. To the audience there was no incongruity in having a white woman explain the basket's symbols, while the weaver herself remained silent. It was, after all, their fantasy."

Despite such activities, it was Abe, not Amy, who was associated with the baskets and Dat So La Lee, although in actual practice his involvement was limited to business aspects such as pricing and advertising. (In 1899, he took several cartons of baskets to San Francisco on his semi-annual clothing-buying trip. He brought along seven Washoe men, to add local color, who unfortunately were promptly cited for loitering.)

Both the Emporium pamphlets and newspapers of the time talked only of Abe; Amy was never mentioned. His picture appeared often, with and without Dat So La Lee, while Amy's was never published. Yet Amy, not Abe, was the basket authority and author of the Emporium articles that spotlighted Abe. Even the basket exhibits at the Nevada and California state fairs in 1900 were her projects. She was a determined woman, and obviously this role was her choice.

Cohodas suggests that her self-denial was part of a promotional package in which Abe was lauded as the generous and long-suffering patron of a brilliant but hopelessly stupid and ugly weaver, who also happened to be the tribal historian. To add to Dat So La Lee's authenticity, the Cohns invented her birth in pre-contact times and had her meet explorer John C. Fremont in Eagle Valley, a place he never visited. But the account served to authenticate Dat So La Lee's role as the keeper of Washoe culture. Abe also "discovered" that Dat So La Lee was actually a beloved and long-lost guardian that he had known at his father's store in Monitor, a small Sierra town; not surprisingly, his father never had a store in Monitor.

And so the fabrications continued. Amy invented Dat So La Lee's technique: The weaver would split her materials with her teeth and fingernails and would, in her resistance to change, use only a broken knife or glass shard to cut them. Despite her obvious lack of mobility, Amy had Dat So La Lee making long treks through the Sierra in search of materials. The prices her baskets brought were also wildly exaggerated.

Dat So La Lee was, in fact, an innovator. When she created the choke-mouthed design known as degikup, it was with new materials and techniques and foreign shapes and motifs. To incorporate this radical change into the mythology, Amy shifted degikup into the pre-contact past. According to Emporium propaganda, the appearance of degikup was due to a Paiute ban on their creation, in effect since 1860. Because Abe (of all people) had promised to protect Dat So La Lee from Paiute reprisal, she (at last) could openly weave such designs, as was her inherited right as a princess, chief's daughter, and medicine woman.

Nowhere did Amy's imagination run freer than with her interpretations of basket designs. For example, her certificate for the burden basket identified as L.K. 51 had this interpretation: "Our men camped beside the roads and rivers, then assembled around the campfires praising and extolling the shrewdness and skill of their hunters in obtaining game of earth and air." For short she called it "Extolling the hunters"—all this despite the weavers' repeated denials that their designs had special messages.

The Cohns' reasons for such inventions ran deep. While the falsehoods were partly for the tourists, Abe and Amy had more complex motives. The other great promoter-seller of Indian baskets at that time was Grace Nicholson of Pasadena. Similar to Amy in strength, background, and interests, Nicholson also patronized talented weavers. Although she didn't interpret or romanticize her baskets, her sales were even greater than the Cohns'—so Amy's inventions may not have helped their sales at all.

For Amy, another motive probably was personal satisfaction. The role that she invented for her husband, especially, was symbolic of the relations between whites and Indians at the time. The Plains Indians had been defeated and confined to reservations, and whites were busy romanticizing the Indians' former culture, using the stereotypes of bonneted warrior and buckskinned princess that survive to this day. Amy dressed this part for her lectures, although her role-playing obviously had little to do with the plight of the Plains Indians and even less with the Washoe. But it had a great deal to do with the white sense of superiority, Cohodas says, and Dat So La Lee therefore served as the scapegoat for white prejudices.

Many Cohn anecdotes were directed at this theme. One that Abe told and retold into legend is about a train trip to St. Louis in 1919, when Dat So La Lee supposedly decided to walk home from Kansas City because she was tired of rail traveling. Another told of her anger when a corset she requested did not turn her into the slim beauty promised in the ad. Her weight, said to be about 300 pounds, was often contrasted with her skilled fingers, as in this description from a 1900 Emporium pamphlet:

"A squaw, whom nature has endowed with considerable avoirdupois, but whose delicacy of touch and artistic ability none can dispute, possessed of childlike blandness, but gifted with much shrewdness and cunning, resorting to romancing and even weeping to gain a desired object. Hand symmetrically perfect, and fingers plump and tapering, she weaves daily her beautiful artistic creations, secretly vain and chuckling at the mere mention of any squaw that can compete with her."

Around 1916 Amy compiled all her certificates in a ledger.

They stated the dimensions of each basket, interpretations of the design, the date or origin, days in manufacture, materials, and techniques. For all its apparent objectivity, the ledger is as suspect as the rest of Amy's data and wasn't even assembled until 20 years after the first basket was made, in 1895. The ledger is a sort of codification of Amy's vision of basketry as a symbol of the romantic pre-contact past.

Her vivid lectures in Indian princess costume, her elaborate propaganda about Dat So La Lee and the baskets, and her vigorous promotion of her husband as the savior of Washoe culture still comprise the biggest source of "information" about Washoe basketry. One of the two major texts on Indian baskets that appeared at the turn of the century, *Indian Basketry*, by George Wharton James, relies heavily on Amy's information. Because of the lack of critical research before Marvin Cohodas, the Cohns' myths have become history.

Amy died in December 1919, and within a year Abe married Margaret Jones, who was more of a traditional housewife and was not very interested in baskets or Dat So La Lee. Later the Tahoe store was closed, and in 1925 Dat So La Lee died.

Even on her deathbed Dat So La Lee was fair game for her exploiters, as Sacramento dentist Dr. S.L. Lee, a basket collector, "revealed" that her name, Dat So La Lee, was taken from his own, "Doc" S. L. Lee, despite its historical use in Washoe as a term meaning "Big Hips." Tootsie Dick, a weaver whom Abe had named as successor to Dat So La Lee, died three years later, and Abe decided to close the clothing business and open an Indian curio store.

After Abe died in 1934, fully three quarters of Dat So La Lee's major works were unsold since collectors had been unwilling to pay what the Cohns knew the baskets were worth.

Margaret sold the baskets off cheaply. One of the three major buyers was the state of Nevada, which got about 20 major pieces for $1,500, or $75 apiece. Today some are worth a quarter of a million dollars each. They are on display at the

Nevada State Museum in Carson City and the Nevada Historical Society in Reno.

By 1935 fancy Washoe basketry was in rapid decline. There are still a few Washoes who learned weaving prior to that time, Cohodas points out, but most no longer weave due to age and arthritis. A number of younger people do the simpler twining, especially for cradleboards, and some non-Indians in the Truckee-Tahoe area practice a coiling technique with pine needles. Cohodas himself weaves fine baskets, but he is adamant that they are his own style, not Washoe. Although the Washoe tribe has shown sporadic interest in a basket revival, with old weavers teaching the young, one bit of Emporium propaganda at least has proved true, long after it was written: that Dat So La Lee was unique, the "last of the great weavers," and that true art in Washoe basketry would die with her.

Thus the historical record has much information about who Dat So La Lee was not, but very little about who she actually was. We know that she was a great artist—her baskets attest to that. Her stitching technique was often incredibly precise. She was an innovator, introducing foreign shapes, design, and materials into her baskets as she made them the basis for elaborate artistic expression.

She must also have been a very strong person, although we have no record of that. She endured humiliation as well as physical affliction. Her relationship with the Cohns, while freeing her to work solely on her baskets, was far from ideal, and her work was all done against the backdrop of the plight of the Washoes in early-20th century Nevada. In spite of this, she became a unique artist, one of the greatest of American Indian basket weavers, and the leader of the fancy basketry movement.

And we still don't know who she really was. We have only a shadowy figure whose baskets speak silently for her, and Amy's legacy: an elaborate fantasy vision of Dat So La Lee at work with her willows.

GASS' STATION

With the arrival of O.D. Gass, 1864 was a pivotal year for Las Vegas—
even though it wasn't yet in Nevada.

(Originally appeared in September/October 1989)

By Ralph J. Roske and Michael S. Green

When Nevada became a state on October 31, 1864, those few souls who lived near what would become the state's largest city really didn't care about Nevada's statehood at all.

The reason was simple: Las Vegas was not yet part of Nevada. Nor would it be until 1867—if then.

Las Vegas would be America's greatest boom town of the postwar era, if not all the time—its metropolitan population has increased from about 8,000 in 1940 to more than half a million today. But in 1864, Las Vegas was barely a one-horse town compared to the Comstock bonanza camps of Virginia City and Gold Hill. Yet it already had a long and intriguing history, and 1864 would be, as it was for Nevada, a pivotal year for Las Vegas.

It was in that year that O.D. Gass rode horseback from San Bernardino to the Mormon mission at St. Thomas, stopping at Las Vegas on the way. Gass, a '49er and former Los Angeles irrigation master, saw enough of the region's possibilities that he would make it his home for most of the next two decades. Indeed, he could be called the first in a long line of Las Vegas' founding fathers.

Thirty-eight years before, Jedediah Smith had become the first white man to penetrate the interior of southern Nevada when in 1826 he traveled near present-day Mesquite along the

O.D. Gass

PHOTO: UNLV SPECIAL COLLECTIONS

PHOTO: UNLV SPECIAL COLLECTIONS

Las Vegas Creek ran near the Mormons' 1855 fort on Gass' ranch.

Virgin River. In 1829-30, leading a trading expedition from New Mexico to Southern California, Antonio Armijo borrowed from Smith and Spanish explorers like Father Francisco Garces to complete the Old Spanish Trail. Rafael Rivera, one of his scouts, may have been the first non-Indian to reach the Las Vegas area, and the Armijo party camped in January 1830 at the mouth of the Las Vegas Wash.

As for much of the West, the great pathmaker for Nevada was John C. Fremont. Before his arrival, Las Vegas had been a slightly known pit stop on the Old Spanish Trail. Visiting the place on May 3, 1844, Fremont noted its warm springs, and his best-selling report on his travels brought new attention to the grassy oasis not far from the Colorado River.

Brigham Young was among those paying attention. To make Las Vegas a part of the Mormon Corridor from Salt Lake City to San Diego, the leader of the Latter-day Saints sent 30 followers to set up a fort-mission that would grow food, serve travelers, and proselytize the Paiute Indians.

Arriving in June 1855, the Mormons built the area's first permanent building—the Mormon Fort, part of which still stands off Las Vegas Boulevard North near Cashman Field. They grew fruit and vegetables, ran water from the nearby creek, and tried to convert the Indians. But the farming founded due to lack of Indian participation, and, more importantly, the discovery of lead at Mount Potosi diverted energies from the mission. After hearing complaints about the harsh climate, alkaline soil, Indian crop raids, and internal squabbling, Young recalled the members of the mission in the spring of 1857, and within two years all had left.

During the Civil War the Union Army spread rumors that the fort had been garrisoned to guard against Confederate raids. While the rumors were untrue, Las Vegas was not a ghost town. Mining continued for a few years at Potosi, and there was a boom in Eldorado Canyon on the Colorado.

One of the original Mormon missionaries, Albert Knapp, decided to return to Las Vegas to take advantage of the mining activity. In 1860 or 1861 he opened a store that served miners and travelers on the Mormon Trail. He then left for California, where he died in 1864.

Albert's interest in the Las Vegas property was inherited by his brother William. Looking for partners, William enlisted a friend who would play a significant role in southern Nevada history: Octavius Decatur Gass.

Gass, who had traveled widely in the Southwest, was a man of varied talents. He spoke Spanish and had acquired some knowledge of civil engineering. Before coming to Las Vegas he sought his fortune in gold and tin mining. Perhaps ranching would satisfy his thirst for success.

Gass was a leap year baby, born on February 29, 1828, and raised on an Ohio farm. He attended Oberlin College, according to his family, although the college has no records of him. Gass traveled around Cape Horn to join the California Gold Rush and later headed for Los Angeles, where he served as water steward. He also invested heavily in tin mines at Temescal in Southern California, but he became embroiled in a controversy over title to the mines. To continue his court fight, Gass needed new funds.

He had enjoyed some success mining in the '50s, so now he

moved to Eldorado Canyon, 40 miles southeast of Las Vegas. Between March 16, 1863, and December 17, 1864, Gass filed 18 mining claims at Eldorado.

"O.D. Gass. . . is the worst-struck man with the prospects here I ever saw," one local miner reported to the *Los Angeles Star.* "I do not suppose he would give a man two bits to ensure him a fortune in the next two years." But fortune would not be his—at least not from mining in southern Nevada.

Meanwhile, Las Vegas was changing territories—from New Mexico to Arizona. By the Compromise of 1850 following the Mexican War, California had become a state and the territories of Utah and New Mexico were created. Las Vegas was part of New Mexico Territory. To add to the confusion, there already was a Las Vegas, New Mexico, so the Mormon Fort's post office was called Bringhurst in honor of the mission's president. In 1863, the Las Vegas area shifted allegiance when the government cut New Mexico Territory in half, creating Arizona Territory, which included present-day southern Nevada.

In 1864, on his trip from San Bernardino to St. Thomas, Gass stopped at Las Vegas. A few years earlier he had met a group of Mormons who informed him that agriculture could be made profitable at "The Meadows."

The desert oasis that Gass first gazed upon 125 years ago may have lacked people but not possibilities. Las Vegas Creek, three feet wide and a foot deep, flowed from the springs and coursed through the valley near the site of the old fort, located on a bluff. Northwest of the mission's adobe-brick walls one could see the remnants of the Indian farm the Mormons had set up in what is now North Las Vegas, land that was later owned by Conrad Kiel, an old friend of Gass' from Ohio.

Amid the sand, grass grew near the spring's creek. The Mormons had proved that between water from the creek and lumber from Mount Charleston, a farm operation was possible.

By the end of 1865, Gass had moved to the Old Las Vegas fort-mission. He and partners Nathaniel Lewis and Lewis Cole, a pair of fellow Eldorado Canyon miners, took over the ranch from William Knapp, who had let the property fall into disrepair while running his late brother's store.

In referring to the ranch, neighbors and even Gass, who knew Spanish much better, called it Los Vegas Ranch. That probably was meant to differentiate it from Las Vegas, New Mexico, or it simply may have stemmed from an indifference to the niceties of Spanish grammar.

In time Gass used two buildings that were joined by a rock-and-adobe wall. The larger one was the residence, and the other was used as a milk house. Other buildings were added later, including a livery and a blacksmith shop. Gass held the "undivided" part of the Las Vegas Ranch, which consisted of only 160 acres as late as 1872. In the mid-'70s the pioneer rancher bought out his two partners and eventually expanded his holdings to 640 acres.

Gass the rancher soon became Gass the family man. His bachelor ways ended after he met Mary Virginia Simpson, daughter of a Civil War officer who was a Missouri miner. Unusually tall for a woman of the 19th century, she stood five feet, eight inches in height and had brunette hair. She was about 30, and unmarried, when she took a railroad trip west with her sister, Ann Jennings. They were met by Ann's husband Isaac in Ogden and then traveled the Mormon Trail. Unable to cross the Colorado River at Eldorado Canyon, they took refuge at Las Vegas Ranch, where Gass had time to make Mary Virginia's acquaintance.

Perhaps at Gass' urging, the Jennings bought land from a Moapa Valley Mormon who was returning to Utah. With Mary Virginia ensconced on a farm near St. Thomas, Gass courted her, regularly making the 120-mile round trip. Finally, Mary Virginia married O.D. at Pioche, the county seat, on February 24, 1872.

At the ranch Gass built an irrigation system and normally grew two crops each year. The first was of small grains such as wheat, oats, and barley. Local Paiutes, for wages in kind, harvested the grains. After the first harvest they planted the fields in cabbages, onions, potatoes, beets, melons, corn, and pink Mexican beans. About 60 Paiutes harvested these crops in the fall. Gass made wine for himself and for sale to travelers. His orchards grew figs, apricots, apples, and peaches. To live as the Gasses did in the Las Vegas Valley was to live in sometimes uncomfortable silent isolation. Indeed, Gass tried to sell his ranch in the late 1870s. Besides trying to pay for his tin-mine litigation, he also recognized that his growing family—the Gasses would have seven children—was rather isolated in the desert he was trying to make bloom.

They were far from schools and stores, visiting only with the few nearby ranchers and with travelers from the trail. They were forced to cope with the scorching heat of the summer. They also had to deal with the Indians who usually were friendly and served as ranch hands. But in 1878 rumors of Indian displeasure prompted Gass to load his children and pregnant wife into a covered wagon and flee to the mining town of Ivanpah, 40 miles west. When he returned, all was well and the ranch was under control of his employees, but the situation reminded the Gasses of their tenuous position. The sale of small grains, fruits, and vegetables and his horses and cattle helped financially, but they led neither to safety nor to the creation of a town.

At the ranch, Mary Virginia was helped by Paiute women with the cleaning and washing. The cooking was done by a Bavarian farmhand or a Chinese cook who was the first Oriental to live in the Las Vegas area. Despite all the help Mary Virginia found much to do. She sewed a great deal, left-handedly; she was ambidextrous in most things. She kept a shotgun handy and would gun down hawks preying on her chickens.

Gass had other interests in the area, particularly in the Mormon port of Callville on the Colorado River. The year 1864 marked the beginning of Callville's short-lived development.

The Church had decided to extend its missionizing activities into what is now southern Nevada, renewing interest in the Muddy and Virginia Rivers. The Mormons wanted to raise cotton, which Southern secession had left in short supply, and to counter non-Mormon miners in the vicinity. They hoped that a port would serve as a gateway to and from southern Utah. Brigham Young wanted to bring goods and converts to Utah from Europe by way of the Isthmus of Panama and the Gulf of California and then up the Colorado.

Young dispatched a bishop, Anson W. Call, who chose a spot that is now beneath the water of Lake Mead at Callville Bay. The Mormons built a stone warehouse and waited and hoped, but to no avail. Callville was too far up the Colorado—steamboats couldn't navigate the sandbars—and mining had slowed somewhat in Eldorado Canyon. Only a few steamships made the trip.

In 1867 Gass became postmaster there and held the job until the post office and Mormon interests in Callville were discontinued in 1869.

In the meantime, though, Gass apparently invested money in the Callville project. Starting a long line of boosterism that has continued in the Las Vegas area, he wrote to the *Arizona Miner* in Prescott, "Since it has been fully demonstrated that the Colorado is fully navigable to Callville the rapid accumulation of steamers for this trade will astonish the most sanguine." Of course, steamers did not rapidly accumulate, but Gass kept promoting Callville, and Arizona newspapers of the time listed him as a Callville resident though he resided at the Las Vegas Ranch.

By 1867, Callville had lost its status as the seat of Pah-Ute County, Arizona. By 1869, the port had been abandoned, and it was so desolate that three horse thieves were able to steal the heavy wooden doors from the stoneware house and use them to build a raft and elude their pursuers by sailing down the Colorado.

While promoting the virtues of Callville, Gass also served in Arizona's territorial legislature. He helped set up Pah-Ute County in what is now southern Nevada and represented it successively in both houses, even serving as presiding officer.

Arizona editors and politicians generally liked and respected Gass, but he soon found he was in the wrong legislature. On May 5, 1866, Congress switched Pah-Ute County from Arizona to Nevada, making it the southern tip of Lincoln County, which also was expanded to the east with lands from Utah Territory.

Gass and his Arizona friends were distraught. They asked Nevada's legislature to create Las Vegas County out of southern Lincoln County, but their pleas were ignored. Then Lincoln County officials demanded that Gass pay them back taxes, which he owed from a period when he tried to keep his holdings a part of the Arizona Territory. The Mormon settlers along the Muddy and Virginia rivers had returned to Utah when they found that they were a part of Nevada, depriving Gass of some of his customers. He remained burdened by the tin-mine litigation and his growing ranch, and the only political office he was able to obtain was justice of the peace.

In 1876, Gass mortgaged the ranch to his old friend and neighbor William Knapp and ended up selling some of his California holdings to pay the debt. In 1879, he arranged a loan from wealthy Pioche rancher and businessman Archibald Stewart, and they later renegotiated the agreement.

However, when the notes came due on May 2, 1881, Gass was unable to settle, and he and his family left Las Vegas the following month.

The Gasses moved to California, where O.D. farmed and mined without much success almost until his death on

December 10, 1924, an event that passed unnoticed in the Los Angeles newspapers and which the *Las Vegas Age* mentioned only briefly in an inaccurate obituary.

Through many of his years at Las Vegas, Gass was a reluctant Nevadan. And yet it might be said that he remained an Arizonan without knowing it. The Nevada Legislature was happy to accept the addition of southern Nevada, and it did so unanimously in 1867. But the Nevada Constitution was left unchanged. Not until 1982 was it amended so that Las Vegas was officially a part of Nevada.

It may seem that the 1860s, so dynamic in western Nevada, were insignificant in southern Nevada. After all, the area remained largely unsettled, and for the bulk of the decade— or, to be painfully precise about it, for more than a century, although for good reason nobody argues the legal point—it wasn't even a part of the state.

But several important seeds had been sown. Octavius Decatur Gass proved to be the first permanent settler at Las Vegas, and after him Archibald Stewart, his survivors, and their friends and employees would remain at the ranch until the building of the San Pedro, Los Angeles, and Salt Lake Railroad would lead to the auction that established Las Vegas on May 15, 1905. And Gass began a long tradition of booster-ism and promotion in Las Vegas that would bear rich fruit in the decades after his death.

Today, Las Vegas is Nevada's largest city, a tourist mecca of world renown. In 1864, when Nevada achieved statehood, Las Vegas was a one-horse town—and, in fact, wasn't even a part of the state. O.D. Gass would be proud.

RAIL DAZE

The Carson & Colorado Railroad was said to be "either built 300 miles too long or 300 years too soon," but its spirit was right on track.

(Originally appeared in Nevada's *125th Anniversary Issue, 1989)*

By Phillip I. Earl

The Carson & Colorado Railroad operated between Mound House, a station on the Virginia & Truckee five miles east of Carson City, and Owens Lake in central California from 1883 until it was sold to the Southern Pacific in 1900. The line was originally built to serve the soda and borax operations in California and to tap the booming mines of Candelaria and Bodie. That boom was over by the early 1890s, however, and traffic dwindled to a trickle by the turn of the century.

Darius O. Mills, one of the backers of the C & C, was once quoted as saying the railroad "was either built 300 miles too long or 300 years too soon." Jim Butler, the original locator of

PHOTO: NEVADA HISTORICAL SOCIETY

Carson & Colorado crews often stopped the train to go rabbit hunting.

Tonopah's rich silver mines, was said to have characterized the line as "the first road he had ever heard of that began nowhere, ended nowhere, and stopped all night to think it over."

The Carson & Colorado was indeed a leisurely and highly informal operation. A trip down the line was nevertheless a memorable experience—shimmering mirages, trackless desert wastes, colorful characters who boarded along the way, and whole Paiute families who rode free as a condition of allowing the tracks to cross the Walker River Indian Reservation.

The southbound run would pick up cans of fresh milk at Wabuska for delivery at various stations, where local residents would stroll down to meet the train and claim their cans on the station platform. Locomotive tenders hauled water for the Indians living near Rhodes Salt Marsh, and company officials once provided a boxcar to serve as a jail there until eight prisoners tore it apart in a successful escape.

As early as 1895, the train of three coaches would often leave Mound House without a single paying passenger. If there was a guest, particularly a young woman, she became the object of the attentions of the conductor, the brakeman, the postal clerk, the express messenger, and the baggage man from the start.

If the passenger happened to be a man, he had to play cards. Should he be unfamiliar with pedro, poker, or placenote, he was compelled to learn. Only clergymen were exempt from this rule. When the crew was absorbed in a game, the train would sometimes miss a station or leave passengers behind at a dinner stop, but these were matters of little consequence since there was plenty of time to back up and no danger of meeting another train.

Coming north out of Hawthorne, it was the custom of the crew to halt the train just out of town and go for a swim in Walker Lake. The sole passenger one day was Mrs. John M.

Campbell, wife of the editor of the *Walker Lake Bulletin.* Reading a book in the passenger coach, she took no notice of the stop but got out to investigate when the delay seemed overly long. Finding the crew skinny-dipping in the lake, she went back to her seat, but she informed her husband of the incident when she returned home. He mentioned it in his next issue and brought it to the attention of the C & C's general manager, Henry M. Yerington, who ordered the practice stopped.

The crews were known on other occasions to interrupt their journeys to hunt ducks and rabbits or join a maintenance crew in tracking quail or grouse. They kept up on the latest word as to the success of local anglers and would pause for a few hours on occasion to try their luck fishing.

Such was railroading in days gone by.

WHERE'S THE BEEF?

How could anyone rustle all those Elko County cows without leaving
a human footprint? Crazy Tex knew.

(Originally appeared in January/February 1990)

By Howard Hickson

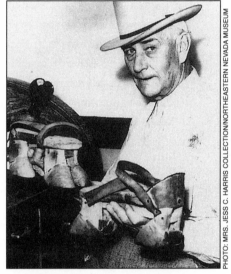

Joe Harris, Elko County sheriff from 1910 to
1936, shows Tex's secret shoes.

Leaning on one knee and
staring at the ground the
buckaroo removed his bat-
tered hat and scratched his
head. Then he and his partner exchanged puzzled looks
as they climbed into their saddles and began to follow a
trail of cow tracks.

A couple of cows carrying
the UC brand were missing,
and it wasn't the first time.
Several head of cattle, one or
two at a time, had disap-
peared over the past few
months. The outfit's riders
suspected that a rustler was on the loose, but they had found
only cow tracks when they investigated. A couple of times
butchered remains were discovered about a mile from where
the animals had disappeared, but there were no human footprints. A lot of people were scratching their heads over the
mystery of the missing cows.

Following this newest trail were two Bills. One was William
Van Eaton, better known as Sanitary Bill, the dirtiest fellow on
the ranch. The other was Cold Water Bill, who, when asked
what he wanted to drink, always replied that a little cold water
would do. They worked for the huge Utah Construction
Company ranch that spread across most the northeastern

corner of Nevada. The trail the two men were following was about 40 miles north of Wells.

"Can't figure it out," Sanitary said. Cold Water shook his head. "Me neither," he said. "Them critters are just plain gone. No sign of 'em—just hoof prints."

They followed the tracks about a mile and lost the trail in a dry creek bed. Then they circled the area until Cold Water picked up a faint trail of cow tracks heading north.

Topping a hill in horse-tall sagebrush, Sanitary grabbed Cold Water's arm and pointed, "Look! That's them! And there's a feller driving 'em on foot." Both horses felt the sting of spurs and carried the two Bills thundering down the hill.

The startled beef thief saw the riders and started running, only to stumble and fall. Bill and Bill reined up in a cloud of dust and pulled their guns on the felonious cattle drover.

It was Crazy Tex. Some people knew him by his real name, J.R. Hazelwood, but many probably had never asked him what it was. Although it was the late 1920s, a man could still get himself killed nosing into the background of another, and the Old West tradition of privacy was respected.

But folks around Elko County knew Tex's habits all too well. Tex, as one buckaroo described him, was "one stave short of being round."

For years he had roamed the vast land of the UC ranches living like a wild animal in caves or in crude shelters he built from willows. No one liked him, and no outfit would hire him. His reputation for erratic behavior kept him from being on any payroll as a buckaroo.

Times had been doubly bad for Crazy Tex. He couldn't get a job if he wanted to, and Prohibition had been law for 10 long, dry years. When UC cooks heard he was on the ranch, they locked up all the vanilla and lemon extract.

Flat on his back, he looked up at his captors. "Hi, fellers!" he said as they dismounted. "I didn't think a big outfit like yours would miss a couple of cows. Needed some dough for grub and a couple of bottles. Didn't think they'd send anybody after me."

Cold Water grimly cocked his pistol and said, "Shut up, Tex. We've wasted damn near half a day on you. Hey—what the hell are those things on your feet?"

Sanitary grabbed one of Tex's feet and held it up. "I'll be damned! You ever see anything like this?"

Strapped to Tex's low-heeled boot was a board, and on its underside two cow hoof were sturdily fastened. His other boot was adorned with a twin to the contraption.

As the Bills inspected his handiwork, Tex admitted that he had practiced walking like a cow for long hours on his hoof-shoes. In fact, he had perfected his length of stride to such an extent that experienced trackers thought it was that of a walking cow. For more than six months he had stolen cattle and robbed coyote traps, always getting away scot-free.

Chuckling, Cold Water commented that it was no wonder they hadn't found any human footprints at the scenes of the crimes.

Tex was lucky that he hadn't been caught rustling 30 years before. Back then, a theif was often hanged from the nearest tree or shot on the spot.

Instead, Sanitary and Cold Water took him back to ranch headquarters, where the cow boss telephoned Sheriff Joe Harris in Elko. Harris drove out to the UC to collect the inventive rustler.

Tex was convicted and spent a couple of years in prison. When he was released, he headed back to the UC and remained a nuisance for several more years. He died in 1953 at age 72, shot by a feuding neighbor while sitting in his pickup truck at Contact.

Tex's unusual hoof-shoes are on display in the Northeastern Nevada Museum in Elko. It may never have crossed his mind that he had rustled cattle using one of the most unique methods ever recorded. Crazy Tex? Perhaps crazy like a fox.

NEVADA'S HISTORIC ARCHITECT

A man of classical visions, Frederick J. DeLongchamps
helped shape Nevada's architectural legacy.

(Originally appeared in July/August 1994)

By Ronald M. James

When the citizens of Las Vegas dedicated the new Clark County Courthouse in 1914, they gave Frederic J. DeLongchamps an ovation as he rose to speak during the ceremonies. The Reno architect's remarks were brief. The *Las Vegas Age* reported, "He said that oratory is not in his line and that he preferred to let the building he had designed speak for him."

It was a characteristically humble response from the man who, more than anyone else, can be called Nevada's historic architect. During a career spanning nearly 60 years, DeLongchamps designed more than 500 buildings. Most major streets in Reno and several rural towns in the state have buildings of his design. He designed seven of the 34 county courthouses constructed in Nevada and planned additions to the State Capitol.

Frederic J.
DeLongchamps

PHOTO: NEVADA HISTORICAL SOCIETY

DeLongchamps' designs reveal a versatile artist who was willing to accommodate the people with whom he worked. The late Reno architect Edward Parsons remembered DeLongchamps as "a personable type of fellow, very charming almost to the point of being disarming, purposeful and very clever. He would, when he met you on the street, change step in order to walk in step with you. A fine character and a great man." DeLongchamps' striving for harmony—working well with clients and designing buildings that blended in—became his hallmark as a professional and private person.

Despite his long and celebrated career, DeLongchamps remains an enigmatic figure. People who knew him said he was nice but could offer few details. It was as if the man succeeded, as he apparently wished, in receding from history's view, leaving only his buildings to speak on his behalf.

And speak they do. The spectrum of his work illustrates several styles as architectural fashion changed over the years. His designs produced sturdy structures that were not cutting-edge but rather explored options within accepted standards. For example, his neo-classical courthouses were conventional, solid buildings that used columns, domes, and other elements from Greek and Roman architecture in ways that shocked absolutely no one.

More than anything else, DeLongchamps had a knack for giving people what they wanted. His buildings have survived longer than most because they immediately became comfortable, like an old shoe.

The architect who brought so many classical buildings to Nevada was born, raised, and educated in the young railroad town of Reno. Born on June 2, 1882, DeLongchamps was the second of five children. After graduating from Reno High in the class of '00, he attended the University of Nevada, where his artistic ability won him the position of illustrator for the *Artemisia,* the university yearbook.

Despite his artistic skills and experiences working with his father, a builder, young Fred DeLongchamps had no intention of being an architect—he wanted to be a mining engineer. He graduated from the university's school of mines in 1904, but his doctor told him that his weak constitution—perhaps a reference to weak lungs—could be strained to the breaking point by a strenuous mining career. Young hopes were dashed. Reluctantly, DeLongchamps took an office job as a draftsman with the U.S. surveyor in Reno.

Then came an event that shook the West—the San Francisco Earthquake of 1906. The disaster gave DeLongchamps, like many other ambitious young men, a chance to rebuild a famous city. He became an apprentice to a San Francisco architectural firm as plans poured forth for reconstruction, and he acquired the training and inspiration for a new career.

When he returned to Reno in 1907, DeLongchamps found a state ready for its own building boom. Mineral strikes in Tonopah, Goldfield, Rhyolite, and Ely had revived the state's economy. A series of mining rushes ensued, and Reno, as a mercantile center, cashed in. Several counties discovered the need to build new courthouses and commercial establishments, and wealthy entrepreneurs commissioned palatial residences.

Given the scarcity of architects in the state—Reno's early 20th-century directories usually listed only two or three—DeLongchamps was in a perfect position. In 1907, he entered into a partnership with Ira E. Tesch, a former colleague at the U.S. Surveyor's Office, and met with immediate success. Over the next two years their firm secured commissions for about 30 buildings.

DeLongchamps' personal life blossomed as well. He married Elizabeth Shay of Virginia City in 1907 and settled in Reno. The couple had a son, named Frederic after his father, the following year.

In 1909, at the age of 27, DeLongchamps won a design competition for the Washoe County Courthouse in Reno. Regarded as one of his most impressive buildings, the monumental neo-classical courthouse still serves as an architectural cornerstone for the city.

During the next 10 years, the most prolific of his career, DeLongchamps designed more than 100 buildings. Between 1909 and 1920 he designed courthouses for seven Nevada counties—Washoe (Reno), Lyon (Yerington), Clark (Las

DeLongchamps designed the Clark County Courthouse in Las Vegas.

Vegas), Douglas (Minden), Humboldt (Winnemucca), Ormsby (Carson City), and Pershing (Lovelock). He also created courthouses for the California counties of Modoc (Alturas) and Alpine (Markleeville). He won awards for the Nevada buildings he designed for the 1915 Panama-Pacific International Expositions in San Francisco and San Diego. In 1913 he drew up plans that extended the north and south wings of the State Capitol in Carson City.

In the 1920s and '30s, DeLongchamps designed three major buildings across the street from the Capitol: the State Supreme Court and Library Building, the Heroes Memorial Building, and its twin, the Ormsby County Courthouse. A similar DeLongchamps "building park" sprang up in Reno around the Washoe County Courthouse. Next door, the Riverside Hotel was built from DeLongchamps' plans in 1927, and seven years later his monumental art-deco Reno Post Office went up across Virginia Street. He also designed structures for the University of Nevada campus, including the Mackay Science Hall and the Scrugham Engineering Building.

He apparently was friendly with such public figures as Governors Tasker Oddie and James Scrugham, likely sharing with both men a love for Nevada mining and history. In 1919,

Scrugham, then state engineer, appointed DeLongchamps to the newly created position of state architect. Although Governor Emmet Boyle dissolved the office in 1921, Scrugham resurrected DeLongchamps' position two years later when he became governor. The state architect's office was abolished in 1926, but not before DeLongchamps had left his creative stamp on the capital.

His wife Elizabeth died in 1924. Two years later he married Rosemary Galsgie of Des Moines, Iowa, who brought a son, Galen, to the marriage.

Over the years DeLongchamps seemed to enjoy taking part in civic and professional groups. He became president of the Reno chapter of the American Institute of Architects. He belonged to the Elks and the Rotary Club. He served two years as president of the University of Nevada Alumni Association. In 1942, ever the mining enthusiast, he was chairman of the local chapter of the American Institute of Mining Engineers.

In 1939, DeLongchamps began a formal partnership with

DeLongchamps' Washoe County Courthouse and Riverside Hotel are Reno landmarks.

George L.F. O'Brien, an architect with whom he had worked occasionally since 1916. O'Brien had a head for business and handled most of the practical aspects of the firm. Artistic creativity was left to DeLongchamps, who retained control of all designs produced by the office.

The DeLongchamps-O'Brien partnership continued until their concurrent retirement in 1965. Four years later, on February 11, 1969, DeLongchamps died in a Reno nursing home.

Many people who knew DeLongchamps typified him as friendly but were unable to add any details or colorful anecdotes. Jack Means, who spent the first years of his career as a staff engineer with DeLongchamps and O'Brien, remembered DeLongchamps as "the finest gentleman I have ever known, someone who never had an unkind word about anybody."

Nevertheless, some clues to the great architect's nature persist. During the Depression his firm's employees complained they were not being paid on time. DeLongchamps, it seems, was using funds to develop mining claims. From 1947 to 1950 he even served as an official in a Comstock mining company. His colleagues recalled that old-time miners would often visit DeLongchamps, looking for a grubstake.

Associates also remembered DeLongchamps' burning desire to be creative. On work days he would rise at two or three o'clock in the morning and walk downtown along the peaceful tree-lined streets of Reno. He would have breakfast at the Palace Club or Golden Club and then go to the office.

The quiet, early hours gave him time for artistic expression. Jack Means recalled that when work was slow, the boss would write poetry or essays. One way or another, his creative drive needed an outlet. One can imagine Fred DeLongchamps sitting alone in his office during those pre-dawn hours, poring over plans for a courthouse, wrestling with columns and archways, long before Reno awoke.

TEN GREAT PERFORMANCES

Stars have made show-biz history in the Silver State.

(Originally appeared in January/February 1995)

Twain. Wayne. Barbra. John, Paul, George, and Ringo. The Rat Pack. The Grateful Dead. Over the years, the biggest names in show business have performed in Nevada and occasionally conjured a little entertainment magic. The following are a few memorable performances that have become part of Nevada entertainment lore.

Ringo, John, George, and Paul greet fans upon their arrival in Las Vegas in 1964.

PHOTO: LAS VEGAS NEWS BUREAU ARCHIVES

1 **Artemus Ward.** Humorist and lecturer Artemus Ward appeared at Maguire's Opera House in Virginia City in December 1863. With his homespun wit and caustic tongue, Ward made a big impression on everyone in the audience, including *Territorial Enterprise* reporter Mark Twain, who was so inspired that a month later he made his first appearance as a lecturer in front of a Carson City crowd. The talk was a huge success and marked the beginning of Twain's remarkable career as an entertainer.

2 **Emma Nevada.** The Silver State's first significant homegrown entertainer was Emma Wixom, who gained international fame in the 1880s as the opera singer Emma Nevada. Emma grew up in Austin, and her talents were first noticed when she sang with a local church choir. Later, she had great success as an opera star in Europe. On December 7, 1885, she made a triumphant homecoming trip to Austin, performing to standing-room-only crowds in the Methodist Church.

3 Ted Lewis. Nevada's first big-name headliner didn't perform in Reno or Las Vegas but at the Commercial Hotel in Elko. On April 26, 1941, bandleader Ted Lewis, a major 1930s and '40s radio and recording star, began a one-week stand at the Commercial for which he was paid $12,000. There was no cover charge, no food, and beers were a nickel. Unfortunately, Lewis, who loved to gamble, lost more than he earned during his stay at the Commercial and had to sign an IOU promising to perform again to settle his debts (which he did later in the year).

4 Lena Horne. While African-American performers had appeared before in Nevada (including the Mills Brothers at Las Vegas' Nevada Biltmore in 1946), Lena Horne was the first to headline at a major hotel when she appeared at Bugsy Siegel's Flamingo in January 1947. The first racially integrated major resort was the Moulin Rouge in Las Vegas, which opened in May 1955 with the "Tropi-Can-Can" floor show that included young dancers Maurice and Gregory Hines.

5 Elvis Presley. Long associated with Las Vegas as an entertainer, Elvis bombed when he first performed at the New Frontier in April 1956. Elvis' teen followers were too young for the Vegas scene, and he was too loud for the older folks. His audience had finally grown up by the time he made his triumphant return to Las Vegas—to sold out showrooms—in 1969.

6 Lido de Paris. The first revue featuring rows of dancing, sequined showgirls was Lido de Paris, a show imported from Paris. The Lido opened in July 1958 at the Stardust Hotel in Las Vegas and ran until 1991. The longest-running revue is the "Folies Bergere," which has played at the Tropicana since 1959. The first topless revue in a major hotel was "Minsky's Goes to Paris," which opened at the Dunes in 1957.

7 The Rat Pack. Few nights have been as magical as the three-week period in January 1960 when Frank Sinatra, Sammy Davis Jr., Dean Martin, Joey Bishop, and Peter Lawford, collectively called "the Rat Pack" or "the Clan," performed nightly during the "Summit Meeting at the Sands." The five entertainers, among the biggest names in show business in the early 1960s (hence the "summit" name), were in Las Vegas to film the movie *Ocean's Eleven* and mesmerized their audiences with impromptu humor and songs.

The Rat Pack at the Sands: Peter Lawford, Frank Sinatra, Dean Martin, Sammy Davis Jr., and Joey Bishop follow the Copa Girls' cue cards.

8 Wayne Newton. No entertainer has performed in Nevada as frequently as Wayne Newton. In 1959, while he was still a 16-year-old high school student, he signed a five-year contract with the Fremont Hotel. Newton has performed thousands of times in the Silver State.

9 Barbra. In 1994, Barbra Streisand made her first live appearance in more than two decades at the opening of the MGM Grand, the world's largest hotel. Streisand has a long history with Las Vegas. In 1963 she made her Nevada debut at the Riviera in Las Vegas as the opening act for Liberace, and in 1969 she headlined at the grand opening of the International Hotel (today the Las Vegas Hilton).

10 Grateful Dead. While it wasn't their first appearance in the state, this classic '60s rock band trucked into Las Vegas' Silver Bowl on April 27, 1991, for two sold-out concerts that attracted more than 79,000 Deadheads, making it one of the biggest rock shows in the state's history. Other successful rock-band debuts include the Beatles, who performed two sold-out shows in August 1964 at the Las Vegas Convention Center. Pat Boone sat in the front row during their first show.

LEADING LADIES

Lawmakers Sadie Hurst and Frances Friedhoff led the way in changing
the all-male club of the Nevada Legislature.

(Originally appeared in March/April 1995)

By Dana R. Bennett

On Election Day in 1918 the *Nevada State Journal* took an unusual stand: The newspaper endorsed a female candidate for the State Assembly. No woman had ever served in the Nevada Legislature. In fact, women were not allowed to vote in state elections until 1916.

Nevertheless, the Reno paper reminded its readers that Republican candidate Sadie Dotson Hurst "has taken an active part in public matters" and assured them that her experience in club work "will stand her and the people of Nevada in good stead should she be elect- ed to the assembly." Washoe County voters apparently agreed, electing Hurst as one of their seven representatives for the 1919 session in Carson City.

Sadie Hurst was Nevada's first female legislator.

Hurst thus became the first woman elected to the Nevada Legislature and a trailblazer for women like Frances Friedhoff, a Yerington rancher who became Nevada's first female state senator in 1935. Although their terms were brief, Hurst and Friedhoff opened important political doors for women in the Silver State. Today, one third of Nevada's lawmakers are female, and it is no longer a novelty for a woman to be elected to the State Legislature.

Hurst's election in 1918 reflected the growing political presence of women in America. Women had been agitating for the vote since 1848 and played crucial roles in the anti-slavery movement. They were the force behind turn-of-the-century laws designed to combat poverty and the drive to outlaw alcoholic beverages. In 1890 Wyoming became the first state to grant women the right to vote, and in 1896 the nation's first women legislators were elected in Colorado.

In Nevada, women were involved with the legislature from the beginning. Hannah K. Clapp of Carson City lobbied the Territorial Legislature (1861-1864) to improve education. In 1877 Mary E. Wright of Virginia City became the first female legislative clerk. But it wasn't until November 1914, following a hard-fought, 45-year battle in the legislature, that Nevada women won the right to vote in state elections.

Sadie Hurst, like many other Nevada politicians, was part of the social reform movement known as Progressivism, which was then sweeping the country. Although details of her early life are sketchy, it is known that Hurst was born in Iowa in 1857 and moved to Reno with her two sons after the death of her husband. In Reno she became involved in women's civic clubs and community improvement projects, both Progressive hallmarks.

Her preoccupation, however, was another Progressive proposal—Prohibition. Unlike ax-wielding Carry Nation, famous for literally breaking up Kansas bars, Hurst used political persuasion to stop the sale and consumption of alcohol. In those days Reno was the epitome of the Wild West, a center for easy divorces, championship prizefights, and back-alley card games. But the public's interest in moral reform and concern about supplies during World War I—grain was better used for food than booze, ran one argument—were strong during the 1918 election. Remarkably, Reno-area voters elected an entirely "dry" delegation, including Hurst, to the legislature.

"I am pledged to but one thing and that is to vote for the

PHOTO: DAUN BOHALL COLLECTION, NEVADA DEPARTMENT OF MUSEUMS

Sadie Hurst (center-right) watches Governor Emmet Boyle sign a resolution ratifying the 19th Amendment, which gave women the vote nationally, on February 7, 1920.

ratification of the federal prohibition amendment," Hurst told the *Carson News.* "Of course," she added, "I am particularly interested in legislation that will be of benefit to women and children."

She continued reassuringly, "I shall be deeply interested in and stand for all legislation that appeals to me to be for the best good of the state. I expect to be quite conservative in my views and certainly have no desire or intention to revolutionize the affairs of the state."

Indeed, Hurst was not a social rebel. She was careful to separate herself from other Nevada women activists, most notably Anne Martin, a candidate for the U.S. Senate in 1918. One of Hurst's campaign ads stated, "Not a member of the Woman's Party," referring to Anne Martin's organization. Apparently Hurst wanted to ensure that no voter would mistake her for a radical feminist.

Early in the 1919 session the *Nevada State Journal* remarked that "the woman lawmaker, Mrs. Hurst, has already had the pleasure of seeing some of her legislative propositions take the form of law." In one of its first actions, the legislature, meeting in its chambers on the second floor of the State Capitol, endorsed the Prohibition amendment to the U.S. Constitution. The paper also noted that "Mrs. Hurst's petition to Congress for woman's suffrage" had passed.

The presence of this new Assembly member occasionally mystified the formerly all-male body. "Much discussion goes on in the assembly as to how to address the Hon. Sadie Hurst," the *Journal* reported. "Some call her the assembly woman while others salute her as the 'gentle lady.'" Whatever they called her, "the Washoe delegates are very proud of having a woman delegate."

Chivalry, however, did not stop the male legislators from making fun of Hurst's legislation or excluding her from functions. After she introduced a bill prohibiting cruelty to animals, some legislators arranged a street fight between a badger and a bulldog. Outraged, Hurst rose on the floor of the Assembly to protest this brutal plan, only to find herself the butt of a joke when it was revealed that the "badger" in the covered cage was really a chamber pot.

Near session's end the Journal of the Assembly included this brief but pointed statement: "Mr. Speaker read a communication from the War Department extending an invitation to the male members of the Assembly and Senate to attend a moving picture and lecture at the Grand Theater." Hurst's response to being so clearly excluded was not recorded, but one wonders about the War Department's subject. Was the "gentle lady" considered too frail for the topic?

Despite such obstacles, Hurst sponsored several bills involving women's rights. One would have given a mother control of her children and their estates upon the death of the father, and another would have allowed women to enter into any legal contract. Neither bill passed. A third measure would have required a wife's signature, in addition to her husband's, to deed real estate held as community property. The bill passed the Assembly but was tabled in the Senate, much to the disgust of the *Nevada State Journal.* "The intent [of the bill] was right and just, but the question of deeding mining property was the striker," the *Journal* stated. "It is evident that the state senators are taking no chances on the women upsetting the mining game in Nevada."

Hurst's successful bills included one that increased the penalties for rape and raised the age of consent from 16 to 18 years. Similar legislation had failed in previous sessions. Her bill outlawing animal cruelty was also approved despite the badger-fight prank. Both houses passed Hurst's measure requiring the registration of nurses. Although Nevada was then the only state not regulating the nursing profession, Governor Emmet Boyle vetoed the measure because it did not specify standards.

Hurst was clearly not intimidated into silence by being the only woman in the legislature. As an adamant Prohibitionist, she strongly opposed a bill, which passed, allowing the sale of "near beer" and flavored cooking extracts that contained minuscule amounts of alcohol. As a suffragette, she stood up for women's rights. She also was staunchly conservative, indeed reactionary, on some matters. At the time it was against the law in Nevada and many other states for people of different races to marry. When the 1919 session considered a bill to legalize marriages between Native Americans and Caucasians, it was Hurst who led the floor fight against it. According to the *Reno Evening Gazette,* Hurst "did not believe in the intermingling of races." However, her colleagues were not swayed by her arguments, and the bill passed by a substantial margin.

A year later the legislature met in special session to ratify the 19th Amendment to the U.S. Constitution, which granted the vote to women nationwide. Hurst and other suffragettes made sure enough legislators would be in Carson City to vote for ratification. The Woman Citizen's Club and the Nevada Federation of Women's Clubs arranged for a special car, the *Suffrage Special,* to be attached to the Virginia and Truckee's train from Reno to Carson. Members also offered to drive legislators to the State Capitol.

When the special session opened on February 7, 1920, animated suffrage supporters filled both chambers. *The Carson City Daily Appeal* reported:

"Speaker Fitzgerald announced that because of the historical importance of the event, and because Mrs. Sadie Hurst was the only woman representative in the legislature, he was going to ask her to preside over the house during the passage of the resolution. Mrs. Hurst took the chair and put the question and announced the vote with as much decorum and familiarity with parliamentary usages as could have any of her colleagues of the opposite sex."

Hurst ran for reelection in 1920 but was soundly defeated in the Republican primary. She left Reno two years later with her sons. In 1952, Nevada's pioneering assemblywoman died in Pasadena, California, at the age of 94.

Hurst opened the doors to the Assembly for women throughout Nevada. Nye County sent an assemblywoman, Tonopah attorney Ruth Averill, to the 1921 session. Since then, every Assembly but three has included at least one elected female legislator.

The doors to the Senate, however, were closed tightly against women until 1935. That year Frances Friedhoff of Yerington was appointed to replace her husband, George Friedhoff, who had resigned to take a job with the Federal Housing Administration. She was sworn in as the senator from Lyon County on March 16, 1935. Because the session was nearly over, she sat in the legislature for only 14 days, and her senatorial tenure lasted just over seven months.

Friedhoff, no stranger to politics, was not simply warming an empty chair. Raised in Carson City, she had worked as a teenager in the household of former Nevada Governor R.K. Colcord (1891-1895), a Republican. Friedhoff became a

Democrat, but she later recalled that Colcord, with whom she remained close, was "inspiring, kind, and encouraging."

She married George Friedhoff in 1912, and the couple moved to a ranch outside Yerington. She became active in civic affairs and in the state's Democratic Party. A tall, charming woman with a beautiful singing voice and a talent for public speaking, Friedhoff sold Liberty Bonds during World War I, organized the first 4-H club for girls in Mason Valley, and helped establish the Lyon County Farm Bureau. She led the movement to establish a Yerington library and consolidate rural schools. In 1923 she was appointed to the State Vocational Board of Education, on which she served for 20 years. In 1924 she was elected Democratic national committeewoman from Nevada. When George resigned from the State Senate, Frances was a logical choice to take his seat.

Friedhoff told the *Nevada State Journal* that she was pleased "to know that the people had so much faith in my husband and that they trusted I would carry out his policies." She was savvy enough, however, to retain her own opinions, insisting that she "favored any legislation which was beneficial to the welfare of womanhood" and noting her special interest "in the advancement and betterment of rural schools."

As in Hurst's case 16 years earlier, there was quite a debate over Friedhoff's proper title. The *Carson Appeal* described the dilemma: "Asked if she preferred 'senator' or 'senatoress,' the 'lady from Lyon' answered that it is her understanding that 'senator' is correct." The press obliged, calling her "Senator Mrs. Friedhoff" in most news accounts.

The seating of a woman in the Senate was much more interesting to the state's newspapers than Hurst's election to the Assembly had been. On March 17, 1935, the *Nevada State Journal* trumpeted: "The Senate Ceremoniously Greets First Woman Member of Body." The *Carson Appeal* observed that "the highly accomplished, widely known and universally respected and liked Mrs. Friedhoff enjoys the distinction of being the first member of the fair sex to be a member of the senate of Nevada." The report continued, "The list of ladies who have been elected to the Nevada assembly and who have made fine records in that legislative body is quite long . . . It will be up to Mrs. Friedhoff now to prove that a woman can be every bit as good a senate member as a man—and she will."

Apparently she fulfilled that prophesy. She chaired the Senate Committee on Public Lands, of which her husband had been a member. In legislation, Friedhoff had a perfect success rate: Her only bill, which granted industrial insurance to people working for the Nevada Emergency Relief Administration, was passed. The bill ensured that female as well as male relief workers were protected.

Despite encouragement, Friedhoff declined to run for the seat in 1936. With her husband working in Reno and her son at the university, she had to manage the Yerington ranch, so she chose her business and family over her legislative career. Thirty years would pass before another woman—Helen Herr of Las Vegas—was elected to the State Senate.

After Frances Friedhoff died in 1958 at the age of 63, the legislature memorialized her as "an illustrious standard bearer in the front ranks of woman's battle for political prominence in Nevada." The legislators remembered Friedhoff's own words portraying her devotion to public service: "Not because of public recognition but for the deep-down-inside-me feeling that I did try to do my best to be of service in my little world."

Frances Friedhoff and Sadie Hurst are unique among Nevada's women lawmakers: In their respective houses, they were the first. Both also blazed important political paths for women. Today, when women are elected to the State Legislature, newspapers no longer debate their proper titles.

FACTS ABOUT
NEVADA'S WOMEN LEGISLATORS:

♣ The first woman to sit in the State Senate, Frances Friedhoff of Yerington, was appointed in 1935. The first woman elected to the Senate was Helen Herr of Las Vegas in 1966.

♣ Nine women legislators were initially appointed, four replacing husbands. Only one appointee was reelected.

♣ After 1916, the first statewide general election in which women voted, there have been only four regular sessions with no women legislators—1917, 1931, 1933, and 1947. The first session with more than one woman was 1923, when four women served in the Assembly.

♣ Counties with the most female representatives have been Clark (Las Vegas), 39; Washoe (Reno), 23; and Nye (Tonopah), 10.

♣ Carson City and Douglas (Minden-Gardnerville) are the only counties never represented by a woman.

♣ The first general-election race between two female candidates took place in 1922 in Lincoln County, when Rita Millar beat Genevieve H. Sperling.

♣ The first woman to defeat a male incumbent in the general election was Alice S. Towle of Fallon in 1922.

♣ The first woman native of Nevada in the legislature was Marguerite Gosse of Reno. Born March 13, 1890, in Virginia City, she was elected to the Assembly in 1922.

♣ The first African-American woman legislator is Bernice Mathews of Reno, elected to the State Senate in 1994.

FIRST FATHER-DAUGHTER LEGISLATORS:

♣ The first grandfather-mother-daughter legislators: Senator William J. Bell (Winnemucca, 1906-1914) was the father of Assemblywoman Hazel Bell Wines (Winnemucca, 1934-1936). Today Wines' daughter, Assemblywoman Gene Wines Segerblom (Boulder City, 1992-present), is the third generation of her family to serve in the legislature.

HOW NEVADA BECAME 'NEVADA'

Nevada or Esmeralda? Oro Plata or Washoe? The story of how Nevada
got its name is filled with political and name-making intrigue.

(Originally appeared in March/April 1996)

By Guy Louis Rocha

Leonard O. Sterns knew what he wanted to call his new state,
and it wasn't "Nevada."

"Let us, by all mean[s], christen the State 'Esmeralda,'"
the lawyer from Aurora in Esmeralda County told his fellow
delegates at the 1863 constitutional convention in Carson
City. Sterns continued with a flourish:

"No State of this Union now commences with the letter E—
let us set her up as high alphabetically as she is geographical-
ly, and in natural wealth clothe her with a congenial name;
mount her upon the glorious chariot wheels of American
Union, and my word for it, she will shine the brightest diadem
[crown] of them all."

Of course, the Auroran's plea on behalf of Esmeralda did
not sway the crowd—Nevada was the state's name when it
joined the union in 1864. But the story of exactly how Nevada
got its name has long been shrouded in mystery. The term
"Nevada" came into use sometime between 1776, when Padre
Pedro Font gave the title of Sierra Nevada ("snow-covered
mountains") to Spanish California's towering range, and 1864,
when Nevada became a state. But as Hubert Howe Bancroft
noted in his *History of Nevada* (1890), "How the territory . . .
came to be called simply Nevada, snowy, is not altogether
clear."

"Nevada" was not a homegrown name, which is one reason
for the long-standing mystery. If the residents of the western
Great Basin had had their way, the 36th state might have been
known as Bullion, Carson, Esmeralda, Humboldt, Oro Plata,

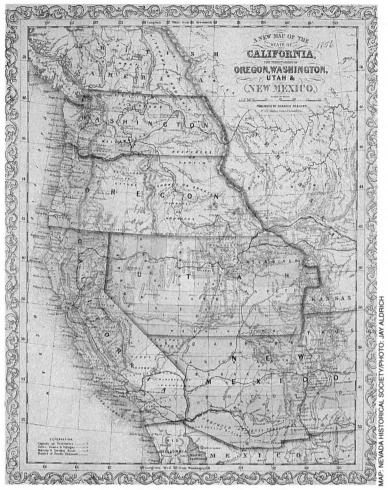

This map shows Utah Territory in 1856. Congress created Nevada Territory
in 1861 and granted Nevada statehood in 1864.

Sierra, Sierra Nevada, Sierra Plata, or Washoe.

Instead, the name "Nevada" seems to have originated in
Washington, D.C., and was first used in 1858, when the House
Committee on Territories christened the proposed territory.
Newly reviewed sources, including House records and bio-
graphical material, tell the story on two levels: not only how
Nevada got its name but also how Nevada came to be a
state. Both processes were intimately linked to the politics of

national expansion and territorial affairs. The creation of Nevada was influenced greatly by the slavery issue, the Mormon question, Indian relations, the approach of the Civil War, and the silver discoveries on the Comstock Lode—not to mention the name preferences of territorial legislators.

Long before the arrival of Spanish, British, and American explorers, Native Americans had their own names for the region we know as Nevada. The Washoes, who lived in and around the Sierra, called their world "Wa She Shu E Deh," meaning "Washoe lands." Other areas were home to the "Numa" (Northern Paiute), "Newe" (Western Shoshone), and "Nuwuvi" (Southern Paiute).

Explorer John C. Fremont gave the region another name. During his expeditions of the 1840s Fremont identified the vast area of internal drainage between the Sierra Nevada and the Rocky Mountains and called it the Great Basin.

Present-day Nevada went by other names before statehood. It was part of Alta California before the end of the Mexican War in 1848, when much of the West was ceded to the United States.

Nevada also was part of Zion, as the Latter Day Saints, or Mormons, called their desert homeland. Based in Salt Lake City, the Mormons established the State of Deseret, a provisional government that included most of what is now Nevada and Utah and parts of seven other states.

To the outside world in the 1850s, Nevada was best known as the western portion of Utah Territory, which Congress created in 1850. The name Utah referred to the Ute Indians, who inhabited its eastern fringe.

Beginning in 1849 the California gold rush brought thousands of fortune seekers across the Great Basin. Traders and Mormon farmers settled in the shadow of the Sierra Nevada, and placer miners came in search of gold. In 1855 the northwestern quarter of present-day Nevada was organized as Carson County by Orson Hyde, a Utah probate judge and one of the LDS Church's Twelve Apostles. Hyde set up his government in Genoa.

Some non-Mormons called the region the Washoe Country, after the Indian tribe, or the Eastern Slope because of its location on the Sierra's east side. Many wanted to give the area yet another name—California. That is, they wanted the Golden State to annex western Utah. Still other residents, disenchanted with the government in Salt Lake City, 600 miles away, called for a separate territory. They weren't sure what to name it, but events proved to be on their side.

By 1857 political affairs in western Utah were in chaos. Orson Hyde, who had alienated many non-Mormons, returned to Salt Lake City, and Carson County was attached to Great Salt Lake County. Devout Mormons trekked back to Salt Lake as Brigham Young, the territorial governor and church president, prepared for a confrontation with the federal government over control of Utah.

That August residents held mass meetings at Genoa. They adopted a resolution asking Congress to create a new territory out of the "Great American Basin." James Crane, an outspoken advocate of states' rights from Virginia and author of *The Past, The Present, and The Future of the Pacific* (1856), was appointed unofficial delegate to Congress.

The proposed territory had various designations. California newspapers sometimes called the area Carson Territory or the Territory of Sierra.

Six months later the region had Congress' attention—and a new name. On February 18, 1858, Crane wrote from Washington, D.C., that, as a war measure directed at the Mormons, "the Committee on Territories has unanimously agreed to report a bill forthwith to establish a Territorial Government out of western Utah, under the name of Sierra Nevada."

Crane's connection on Capitol Hill was William "Extra Billy" Smith, a fellow Virginian who had spent time in California.

Because of his personal agenda, Smith would prove to be extremely impor- tant in Nevada's march to state- hood. A slave owner who support- ed the concept of "popular sover- eignty," Smith favored a policy of U.S. expansion that would allow citizens of new territories to decide if they favored slavery when they pursued statehood. Nevada later became a firmly Union state, but in the late 1850s the region's loyalty was an open question:

William "Extra Billy" Smith

PHOTO: LIBRARY OF VIRGINIA

Would residents of the new territory side with the South or the North? Smith thought Nevada might be good for the Southern cause.

In 1858 the issue of territorial status for western Utah drew Congressman Smith to Crane and his friend, Major William Ormsby, another new arrival in Genoa and a leader in the ter- ritorial movement. All three men were 49ers, and Ormsby apparently had served with Smith's son in William Walker's ill- fated filibustering force in Nicaragua two years earlier. Ormsby was interested in mail lines, as was Extra Billy, who gained his nickname after allegedly receiving extra payments for the U.S. mail routes he operated a few years before. Crane may have known Smith in both Virginia, where Extra Billy was a legislator and governor, and California.

At Crane's request President Buchanan presented to the House on April 9, 1858, a Carson Valley citizens' memorial asking for a separate territory. Smith and the House Committee on Territories responded by shortening the name of the proposed territory from Sierra Nevada to Nevada and outlining boundaries similar to the state's present borders.

This was the first public appearance of the name "Nevada." Smith's committee had shortened the name sometime during late April and early May, but we may never know the reason because there are no committee minutes and the original bill no longer exists.

"The New Territory of Nevada," read a headline in *The New York Times*. The story noted that a bill creating Nevada Territory was to be reported out of committee shortly, but "if there is any disposition to debate it exhibited, it may be thrown over."

William Ormsby
PHOTO: NEVADA HISTORICAL SOCIETY

On May 12, 1858, Extra Billy Smith submitted a committee report supporting the new territory. Members noted the reasons: "to protect the public mails travelling within and through it; make safe and secure the great overland route to the Pacific as far as within its limits; restore friendly relations with the present hostile Indian tribes; contribute to the suppression of the Mormon power by the protection it might afford to its dissatisfied members; and [be] of material aid to our military operations. Thus satisfied and impressed, your committee respectfully report a bill for the formation of a new Territory . . . to be called the Territory of Nevada."

However, most Southern representatives did not want to add another territory, and Congress adjourned in June without taking further action.

In July 1859 the citizens of western Utah forced Congress to act. At a constitutional convention in Genoa the sagebrush rebels declared their secession from Utah Territory. They named their provisional territory Nevada, taking the name advocated by Smith and his House colleagues.

The secessionists faced a setback that fall when the 40-year-old Crane, an articulate spokesman for the provisional Nevada Territory, died of a heart attack in Gold Hill. His place was taken by John Jacob Musser, one of the founders of Carson City. Musser traveled to Washington, where he pressed Nevada's case on members of Congress.

Officials in Salt Lake frowned on the activities of the Carson County insurgents.

"In reference to the difficulties known to exist in the portion of this Territory known as Nevada," proclaimed Utah Governor Alfred Cumming in a February 1860 report to the U.S. Secretary of State, "I believe them to arise from a settled determination on the part of its inhabitants to recognize no courts and obey no laws, except those which have their origin in, and spring directly from primitive assemblages of the people."

The *Salt Lake Mountaineer* ridiculed the separatists and suggested that "each man of the three or four hundred who are citizens of that majestic sovereign territory ought to have an office . . . But do not be afraid, Sister Nevada, we shall not contest your right to a divorce."

While Washington pondered Nevada's fate, other names were being used for the region. Reporting on gold fever and the "rush to Washoe" in the *San Francisco Herald* on March 26, 1860, Richard Allen relayed "the glad intelligence that Western Utah (or Nevada, Carson, Washoe, or whatever it may yet be permanently named) is richer than all the Potosis or El Dorados that have ever yet been opened to the sight of man."

On May 11, the House Committee on Territories reported favorably on a bill to provide a temporary government for the Territory of Nevada. But the bill was soon amended and counter-amended. Some representatives from the border states, including Smith, supported territorial status if slavery was not outlawed in the organic act. Representatives from the Deep South, however, feared Nevada was destined to be a free state. So the bill was tabled.

In the end William Smith, who would soon leave the House

and serve in the First Confederate Congress, voted against creating Nevada Territory.

By the time Pony Express riders had delivered the bad news to the citizens of western Utah, Major Ormsby had met a violent end. On May 12, 1860, he was a casualty of the first battle of the Pyramid Lake Indian War. Despite the loss of Ormsby's leadership, the citizens of western Utah continued to press their case for a Nevada Territory.

They found a more receptive audience when Congress reconvened in December 1860. Several developments—the silver and gold discoveries at Virginia City and Aurora, the need to provide for the safety of settlers, and, most importantly, the coming of the Civil War following the secession of seven Southern states—prompted the remaining members of Congress to pass a Nevada Territory bill. On March 2, 1861, as one of his last actions in office, President Buchanan signed the organic act that finally created Nevada Territory.

So Nevada was the region's chosen name—or was it?

The next year there appeared support for a state to be called "Washoe." Promoters of statehood were not discouraged by the fact that their territory, with its 30,000 inhabitants, did not have the requisite population, about 60,000, to have one member in the House and justify statehood. Thus, optimistic territorial legislators met in Carson City in December 1862 and approved "an act to frame a Constitution and State Government for the State of Washoe."

The name debate came to a head the following November when delegates met in Carson City to draft a constitution. However, as the convention's minutes reveal, many of the delegates objected to the name Washoe.

Alanson W. "Lance" Nightingill of Unionville wanted the new state to be named after his county, Humboldt. That caused attorney Leonard Sterns, the delegate from Aurora in Esmeralda County, to declare that "there is a regal odor about the name of Baron Humboldt that I, for one, am opposed to encircling around the free State of Esmeralda." Baron von Humboldt, a German naturalist, geographer, and world traveler, had never seen the river named after him by John C. Fremont.

"While I pay homage to his worth and to his giant mind, I perceive a decided inappropriateness in his name for us and our posterity," Sterns decried. "Names of men of foreign birth and kingly titles, are not befitting our Republican Government, our democratic institutions." Sterns also attacked the name Washoe, displaying the racism and anti-democratic feelings toward Native Americans so prevalent at the time.

The Aurora attorney futher declared, "Nevada is proposed by some. I had the honor of putting the first article in print advocating that proposition in this Territory; but I have repented, and abandoned my first love for that more endearing one which is named in my report. . . . Nevada is a euphonious name—but how much more so is Esmeralda!"

Unmoved by Stern's passionate remarks, Nightingill withdrew Humboldt in favor of Nevada. By a vote of 32 to four, Esmeralda was thrown out. After an eloquent plea for Washoe by Charles S. Potter, a merchant in the Washoe County settlement of Ophir, during which he defended the good name of the Washoe people, the delegates adopted the name Nevada by a vote of 28 to eight.

Residents voted down the state constitution as a result of mining-tax and election disputes, but national politics put the statehood process back on track. Moderate Republicans wanted to strengthen President Lincoln's position in the 1864 election, a three-way race involving Lincoln; General John C. Fremont, the Radical Republican candidate; and General George B. McClellan, a Democrat. Congress soon passed an enabling act for "the People of Nevada" that paved the way for statehood. Lincoln signed the bill on March 21, 1864. Now it was up to the territory's citizens.

Once again, the naming of the new state aroused animated debate when a constitutional convention met in Carson City that July. Some delegates supported Humboldt and Esmeralda while others suggested such names as Bullion, Oro Plata, and Sierra Plata.

John A. Collins of Virginia City advocated the name Washoe. Collins argued that the name Nevada would cause great confusion because California already had a Nevada City and a Nevada County as well as the Sierra Nevada. Moreover, Collins proclaimed, "those who understand the meaning of the word [snow-covered] are aware that it is wholly impracticable to us. When you hear it, you are inclined to button your coat, and shiver. Here we have an almost semi-tropical climate of almost the whole of the Territory . . . We are known everywhere, north and south, east and west as Washoe."

Charles W. Tozer of Gold Hill challenged Collins' view: "We are already known as the Territory of Nevada and a great part of our Territory lies throughout its course at the base of the Sierra Nevada Mountains. I think it proper to call the State 'Nevada' on that account alone."

"There is another reason why the name Nevada should be retained," declared Nathaniel Ball. A Gold Hill banker, Ball said he had surveyed Eastern visitors on what they called the area. "Without exception, those gentlemen told me that they never heard the name of Washoe applied to this country at all, until they came to California, except by some of their friends who had resided in California," he said. "They each and all assured me that the name by which we are known throughout the East is Nevada."

J. Neely Johnson, president of the convention and former governor of California, made another compelling argument. "In the Enabling Act, as I conceive, Congress had specifically prescribed our name," Johnson pointed out. "Now the child is named; it has been baptized by the name of Nevada, and nothing short of an act of Congress can change that name."

On September 7, 1864, the voters of Nevada Territory approved the constitution by an eight-to-one margin. President Lincoln proclaimed Nevada a state on October 31, a week before the national election. Lincoln easily carried the new state—Fremont had dropped out of the race in September—and Nevadans gave the beleaguered president three Republican Congressmen to help him rebuild the nation.

Thus the Battle Born State had acquired its name only after a long series of skirmishes at home and in the halls of Congress. Given the degree of national politics involved, it seems fitting, if ironic, that our state's name was fashioned in a House committee room rather than a raucous meeting of insurgents in Genoa or Carson City. If it hadn't, what we call Nevada today might be known instead as the great state of Esmeralda, Humboldt, Washoe, or even Bullion.